MIDEAST
&
MEDITERRANEAN
CUISINES

by Rose Dosti

FISHER
BOOKS

Publishers:	Bill Fisher
	Helen Fisher
	Howard Fisher
	J. McCrary
Editor:	Veronica Durie
Cover & Illustrations:	David Fischer
Book Design:	David Fischer
Book Production:	Paula Peterson

Published by Fisher Books
P. O. Box 38040
Tucson, Arizona 85740-8040
602-881-6333

Copyright © 1993 Fisher Books
Printed in U.S.A.
Printing 10 9 8 7 6 5 4 3 2

**Library of Congress
Cataloging-in-Publication Data**

Dosti, Rose.
 Mideast & Mediterranean cuisines /
by Rose Dosti.
  p. cm.
 Includes index.
 ISBN 1-55561-055-2 : $9.95
 1. Cookery, Middle Eastern.
2. Cookery, Mediterranean. I. Title.
II. Title: Mideast and Mediterranean
cuisines.
TX725.M628D67   1993
641.5956—dc20   93-37394
                                      CIP

Table of Contents

ROSE DOSTI

As a seasoned traveler, Rose Dosti became fascinated with the variety and beauty of foods from the Mideast and the Mediterranean and their link to Eastern and Western cuisines in the use of ingredients, cooking methods and style. After each trip to a country, Rose became more aware of the interest and curiosity shown by cooks in the Western world. She realized that the little-known cuisines of the center of the world offered an exciting repertoire for entertaining and healthful family cooking.

Rose has been a food and nutrition writer for the *Los Angeles Times* for over 25 years. She has written on a variety of food-related topics including restaurant reviews, nutrition, chefs' recipes and a reader request column. She is author of several other cookbooks.

INTRODUCTION

When I began collecting recipes during my visits to the Middle East, I realized that Mideast and Mediterranean cooking held the key of understanding to both Eastern and Western cuisines. Without Middle Eastern trade routes, access to ingredients, ideas and culinary exchanges between East and West would not have been possible. Coffee from East Africa, tea from Asia, spices, new foods and cooking methods from throughout the East and Near East would not have found their way to cuisines of the West.

At the same time, the Middle Eastern cuisine was itself a personification of all its influences: East, West and Middle, more so than any other world cuisine.

In working with this book you will also come to the realization that the Middle East cuisine is, indeed, the extending arm that connects the cuisines of the East and West in a perfect, global culinary circle.

HOW IT BEGAN

Earliest civilizations began in the areas fertilized by the Euphrates and Tigris Rivers in Iraq, and by the Nile River in Eygpt. Early man tended wheat fields and domesticated animals. He made bread from seeds and ate mainly grain.

Later, Indo-European tribes such as the Hittites, Persians and Armenians settled in Asia Minor. These meat-eaters added barbecued meats and preserved dairy products, such as yogurt and cheese, to the diet of grains.

Arabs journeying throughout the Middle East and Mediterranean spread not only their language, philosophy, medicine, mathematics and faiths, but new agricultural methods and spices from the Orient.

About the same time the Byzantine, or Eastern branch of the Roman Empire brought delicacy to Middle Eastern cooking. This domination lasted from the 4th to the 15th century. Over the next 500 years Ottomans spread their empire from the Middle East to the Balkan Peninsula in Europe.

The cuisines of the Mideast and Mediterranean contain many mainstay dishes in common with only slight variation. I have tried to maintain the integrity of the original dish as much as possible within the bounds of modern standards of taste and cooking methods.

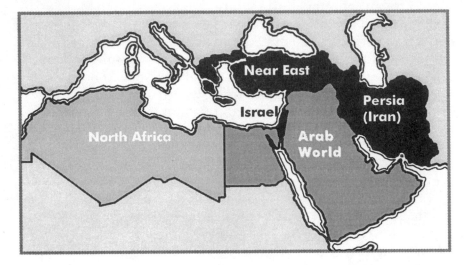

THE FIVE CUISINES

Technological advances of the last 50 years have affected every aspect of society from politics to the food we eat every day. No world cuisine has remained unchanged. New culinary ideas and ingredients make their mark of change continually. However, for culinary focus I have preserved the basic essence of the Mideast-Mediterranean cuisines and customs, using the most well-known recipes of each.

For purposes of this book, the Mideast and Mediterranean cuisines fall into five general spheres, although their influence far exceeds the geographic boundaries set forth here: Persian (known now as Iranian); Arab World, including Iraq, Syria, Lebanon, Jordan, Egypt and the Arabian Peninsula; Near East, encompassing Turkey, Armenia and Greece, representing the highly similar cuisines of the other Balkan nations; North African, which includes Libya, Algeria, Tunisia and Morocco. Israel, bordered by Lebanon and Syria, remains separate from the other areas because its cuisine is based on culinary influences of scores of countries, as well as the indigenous Arab cuisine.

IRANIAN CUISINE

Easternmost Iran, once known as *Persia,* boasts one of the most sophisticated, elaborate and complex cuisines of any in the Mideast. The food of Iran centers around meat, dairy products, rice and aromatic spices and herbs that enhance it.

An Iranian meal may start with a plate of assorted herbs, served with a white cheese, cucumbers in yogurt and bread. The meal always includes a rice dish, soup or a soup-stew, fresh green salad, pickles and yogurt. Sherbets, fruit drinks and desserts are served at the end of the meal. Tea is served after the meal and between meals.

In the Persian cuisine rice is the sun around which satellite dishes revolve and interplay. No meal is without it, nor are violations of its strict role allowed. For example, *chelo,* or steamed rice, is the accompaniment for barbecued meats, not to be mixed with other foods. Rice combined with other foods is called *pollo.* Rice garnished with egg yolk may be served with meat, but not chicken. Meat stews belonging to a category of *khorak* are never mixed with rice, while *khoresht,* the soup-stews, are served with rice.

Legend has attributed the discovery of yogurt to Persians. Yogurt is a basis of an entire category of appetizer-salads called *borani.* A table is never set without yogurt in at least one of its many guises. It can be spooned over rice, meat, fish, poultry or mixed into soups, stews and salad, even breads and dessert.

No cuisine has made more exotic use of herbs. While you may find the Persian approach to herbs rather startling, it's quite adventuresome. Herbs are used in omelets, salads, soups and rice dishes. Herb & Nut Omelet, intoxicatingly aromatic with dill, parsley, cilantro, saffron and cinnamon, raisins and nuts, is a classic example.

Fruit as a versatile ingredient has exceeded anything imagined by Arabic or Ottoman cooks. Prunes are added to Picnic Meatballs. Pomegranate juice is spooned over duckling and flavors soups and stews. Fruit juices are added to sherbets, jams and jellies.

Nan-e-lavash, the dinnertime bread of Iran, is almost identical to Armenian *lavash,* Lebanese *Khbuz Mar'ook* or Indian *Naan.* Paper-thin bread dough is baked against sides of a beehive-like oven called a *tanour* (called *tandour* in India). For a similar effect—and convenience—my bread recipe calls for baking the dough on an inverted wok heated over the range.

ARABIAN CUISINE

The cuisines of the Arabian Peninsula, Lebanon, Syria, Jordan and Egypt are dependably similar. Most foods are known by Arabic names, varying only in spelling and pronunciation.

A wide range exists between a simple meal in a Bedouin's tent on the desert and the elaborate culinary style and presentations of Lebanese and Syrian mastercooks in metropolitan areas. An opulent culinary style was introduced by the Byzantines, then overlapped by the Ottomans, who ruled these Arab lands for over four centuries. But in general, the peoples of the Arab World follow ancient eating habits and use common, basic ingredients.

Ancient man's diet, rich in grains, beans and legumes, still prevails by and large. Beans, especially fava beans, known as *fool*, or *ful*, go back to the days of the pharoahs. In Egypt, the national dish is Fool Medames, eaten morning, noon, and night, as well as an appetizer.

Wheat, the food of the first civilizations of mankind, is still a staple from which various types of flat bread are made. It also provides another popular staple, bulgur, a cracked wheat eaten plain or in salads.

Spices introduced by caravan traders over thousands of years have been ingeniously incorporated into the cuisine. Arab cooks love seasonings. Heady spices such as saffron, cinnamon, cloves, ginger and cardamom are used imaginatively in exotic combinations. Even desserts may contain rose water or orange-blossom water and cardamom to enhance flavor.

Yogurt, known as *laban*, is a favorite thirst-quencher when diluted with water and seasoned with salt.

Sesame-Seed Sauce, or *tahini*, is used over everything, including bread, fish, meat, rice, bulgur, salad and soup. It provides a protein supplement in a chiefly carbohydrate diet.

Kibbe, or *kubbe*, a minced, molded, stuffed or layered ground lamb is basic to the Arabic cuisine. Lamb, in fact, the symbol of hospitality throughout the Middle East, is still served in honor of special guests. It may be roasted inside vertical or horizontal pits to serve whole on a tray with rice, salads, dates, bread and fruit, or made into stews, *kibbes* and *kebabs*.

Foods are usually minced or cut up for easy enclosure in pieces of soft, chewy pocket bread. Eating is mostly communal-style, except in restaurants and hotels and in Westernized cities. While forks and spoons are widely used, fingers are traditional. The Arabic custom of washing hands before and after meals is based on religious tenets of cleanliness which have been practiced for centuries.

NEAR EAST CUISINE

Turks, Armenians and Greeks share a culinary heritage rooted in Byzantine and Ottoman cultures. The high-protein diet is based on cheese, yogurt and meat, chiefly lamb, roasted in a pit or on a spit. *Shish Kebab*, meaning skewered meat, is common to all.

Yogurt is a standard item used as a dressing for vegetables, rice, meats and soups. Turks and Greeks use pita bread and in Turkey's countryside, bulgur is as popular as rice. Cheese, especially white goat cheese, called *feta* in Greek, is often eaten for breakfast with olives and bread. It is used as a filling for savory filo pastries, or as an appetizer on a *meze table*, enjoyed with *ouzo* (a Greek anise-flavored liquor) or *raki* (the Turkish equivalent made with grapes).

Although rice is generally imported, it is considered an integral part of the cuisine. Long-grain rice is preferred and cooked so it is moist enough to savor and dry enough so that every grain is discernible. Sticky rice is generally abhorred.

Few cooks are more imaginative in their use of vegetables than Greeks and Turks. Their kitchens are often fragrant with aromatic herbs, such as dill, basil, mint, oregano, garlic and onion. Eggplant, a native to India brought to the Mediterranean area by traveling Arabs, can be found in national dishes such as Moussaka in Greece and Patilcan Imam Bayildi (fainting Imam) in Turkey.

Filo dishes seasoned often identically are eaten as appetizers or between courses. Fillings range from savory to sweet and new fillings continue to be discovered. In Istanbul, bakeries sell pastry made with chocolate filling wrapped in chocolate filo sheets.

Meals, especially company meals, are generally leisurely,

beginning with the meze or appetizer course. If raki is served, Turks follow meze with grilled meats and a salad. Family meals may begin with a modified meze and proceed to soup, or stew, grilled or baked meats with rice or potatoes. Beverages such as wine, diluted yogurt, buttermilk, water or beer are also served with meals.

The cuisine is rich with lavish desserts. Deluxe Baklava, nut-filled Shredded Pastry Dessert, and pastries dripping with honey syrup reflect a Byzantine taste for sweets that is characteristic of the Middle East.

NORTH AFRICAN CUISINE

The North African countries of Libya, Algeria, Morocco and Tunisia share a common Arabic heritage dating back to Islamic conquests in the seventh century. The cuisine has been influenced by both Arabs and Berbers. Egypt is geographically part of North Africa, but it is totally Arabic in culture. Other North African countries identify only partially with Arabic culture, even though Arabic is the language.

Turkish-Byzantine influences are unmistakable in all the countries, even in Morocco where no Turkish rule existed. The French who left their language and appreciation of French culture made no significant inroads in altering the already rich Moroccan cuisine. French cuisine, although present, remains quite separate.

The Berbers are a major part of the populations of North African countries. As Egyptian tomb paintings suggest, the Berbers are the aboriginal peoples of North Africa. They have managed to retain much of their language and culture, as well as many ancient dishes.

Couscous, for instance, is from the Berber word *kukus*. It is actually semolina, the heart of durum wheat, which has been processed into a pasta grain similar to fine bulgur in texture. It is eaten much the same way as bulgur, but many cooks in North Africa prefer it steamed in a double-boiler pot called *keskes* or *couscousière* in French.

Tajine, another indispensible category of dishes highly influenced by Arabs and the colorful Berbers, is common to all North Africans. In Morocco, the word *tajine* also refers to the cone-shaped ceramic dish in which foods are cooked and served. Tajines are made with fish, meat, vegetables, fresh and dried fruits, nuts and seeds in colorful combinations. Lemon Chicken on page 105 is a tajine recipe.

The bread in Morocco has an Arabic name, *khubz,* but it is more French than Arabic in structure and method of baking. The crust is removed and discarded while only the soft pulpy flesh is consumed, often used to wipe away a crumb from one's lips.

Turkish-style filo pastries are known as *biouats* in Morocco, *breik* in Tunisia and *bourek* in Algeria. They may be filled with meat, vegetables, chicken, salads and even eggs as in the Tunisian dish, *La Breik à L'Oeuf* (Eggs in a Package) on page 112.

One of the great savory pastries of Morocco is *bastela* or *bastila,* filled not so oddly with eggs and chicken and powered heavily with sugar and cinnamon. The dish is so basic to Moroccan menus that it has become a test of deftness for a new bride under her mother-in-law's watchful eye. The heady seasonings of North Africa are similar to America's Southwest cuisine, spicy and hot, often fiery. Algerians, in fact, think Tunisian cooking is too hot. Tunisians regard Moroccan cooking as richer and far more complex than their own.

Coffee is often flavored with rose water in Algeria and orange-blossom water in Tunisia. Moroccans enjoy French-style café noir or café au lait, but minted tea is king. While the ceremonial tea service is fast disappearing from the modern scene, it is still revered by the older generation, who preside at tea, mixing the mint leaves and tasting the brew before it is served.

Few Mideast countries place as much importance to atmosphere as North Africans. In Morocco, dining takes place in opulent comfort with Arabesque-designed backdrops. *Arab rooms,* as they are generally called in Morocco, are lined with divans richly covered with silk pillows. A round table, placed in the far corner where the divans meet, is surrounded by leather hassocks for sitting and, often, lounging.

A meal is not complete without a colorful tray of seasonal fruit artfully decorated with flower blossoms and leaves.

In cities, Western ways of dining prevail. Plates may be stacked at each setting according to the number of courses expected. The appropriate plate is removed after each course. Otherwise, tablecloths layered one over the other are whisked away one by one until the final course is gone. At a North African Arabic-style meal, you begin by washing your hands in a brass, silver or pewter basin. The meal may end with a few drops of rose water or orange-blossom water splashed on the palms of your hands.

ISRAELI CUISINES

Israeli cooking is international because many immigrants from about 100 different countries make up the majority of the population. Sephardic Jews from Greece, Turkey, Spain and North Africa have added a rich roster of dishes. Eastern European Ashkenazi Jews have brought *borscht*, potato dumplings, *gefilte* fish, noodle pudding and ceremonial braided egg bread. Northern European bagels and pretzels could be forms of Sesame Bread rings, the chewy bread sold by street vendors throughout the Middle East. Matzo, flat unleavened cracker-like bread used for Passover meals may be a form of Armenian and Arabic cracker breads.

Dietary laws, called *kashrut*, place many restrictions on food habits. Pork and crustaceans are forbidden. Dairy dishes must be cooked and eaten separately from meat dishes. Dairy foods and meats require separate dishes that must also be used, cleaned and stored separately. Only "neutral" or *pareve* foods, such as fish and eggs, may be eaten with either meat or milk. The Sabbath is considered a day of rest and no cooking is done on that day. Foods that contain no dairy products and may withstand hours of cooking over low heat are prepared overnight to be eaten on the Sabbath.

Meals in Israel tend to be European in style but Middle Eastern in content. Breakfast may include a chopped salad, olives, cheese, pickles, a flat bread for wrapping, and coffee with hot milk. The main meal is at midday with the entire family assembling after shops and schools close. A evening meal may contain a light supper of sardines, dairy products, eggs and salad.

GLOSSARY OF FOOD & DRINK

Most of these foods may be found in Middle Eastern or Mediterranean grocery stores and many supermarkets. Recipes are given where appropriate.

Arabic Pocket Bread, Khubz Arabi *(Arabic)*: the ancient flat bread of the Arabic World. May be opened to form a pocket. Used for sandwiches or to pinch off for scooping up foods. See Arabic Pocket Bread, page 50.

Arack *(Arabic)*; **raki** *(Turkish)*; **ouzo** *(Greek)*: a liquor made from grape juice, grains or fruit in southeast Europe and the Middle East.

Avgolemono *(Greek)*: a sauce made with egg and lemon and used in soups or sauces for vegetables, meat or fish. See Egg & Lemon Sauce, page 40.

Ayran *(Turkish, Arabic)*; **dugh** *(Persian)*: yogurt diluted with water and seasoned with salt or sugar.

Baklava *(Greek, Turkish)*; **baklawa** *(Arabic)*; **paklava** *(Armenian)*: a dessert made with layers of filo pastry, filled with nuts and steeped in syrup.

Basterma *(Armenian)*; **pastourma** *(Greek)*; **pastirma** *(Turkish)*: dried beef similar to beef jerky thickly coated with spices, such as fenugreek, chiles, garlic and paprika. Thinly sliced and used in sandwiches, appetizers or with eggs. Prosciutto may be substituted.

Borek *(Turkish)*; **boureki** *(Greek)*; **bourek** *(Algerian)*; **breik** *(Tunisian)*; **briouats** *(Moroccan)*, **beoreg** *(Armenian)*: pastries made with filo pastry and filled with meats, vegetables, cheese and other savory fillings. See chapter on Filo, page 77.

Bulgur, burghul *(Arabic)*: parboiled and dried wheat processed into grains of varying sizes from fine-grade to coarse-grade. Used like rice.

Chemen, chaimen *(Armenian)*: see fenugreek.

Coffee, kahwa *(Arabic)*; **kafes** *(Greek)*; **kahve** *(Turkish)*: roasted and pulverized coffee beans made into a brew. Pulverized coffee is available in canned form or can be ground in a coffee mill.

Couscous, kuskus *(Berber)*: grains of various sizes made from semolina, the heart of durum wheat, which is coarsely ground, parboiled and dried. Grains vary in size from fine to coarse pellets. The finest grade is used to make the dish called *couscous*.

Dolma *(Turkish)*; **dolmeh** *(Persian)*; **dolmades** *(Greek)*: any food stuffed with meat, rice or other filling.

Fava Beans, fava *(Turkish)*; **fool** *(Arabic)*: a broad bean from the plant of the legume family that bears broad pods with large, flat seeds. Only small fava beans, known as *brown* or *Egyptian brown beans*, are used in making Egyptian Beans, page 64. Any large beans, such as kidney or Great Northern beans may be substituted. Some people with certain enzyme deficiencies may have a toxic reaction to fava beans. If you suspect such a deficiency, avoid eating fava beans.

Falafel *(Arabic)*; **tameya** *(Egyptian)*: fried cakes or balls made with garbanzo or other beans and seasonings. Used mainly as appetizers or in pita-bread sandwiches. Falafel mix is available in package form.

Fenugreek: a plant of the legume family native to southeastern Europe and west Asia. Ground seeds called *chemen* in Armenian and *hilbeh* in Arabic are used as a seasoning. Ground seeds or powder are available.

Feta *(Greek)*: a semi-soft salty white cheese made with goat's milk or sheep's milk. Sold in cans, cut in brick shapes or in vacuum-sealed packages. Usually stored in brine. Ricotta, dry-curd cottage cheese, hoop cheese, pot cheese or any semi-soft Mexican-style cheese may be substituted.

Filo, phyllo *(Greek)*: a paper-thin sheet of dough used to make sweet and savory pastries. Available in rolls of 10 to 20 sheets at Middle Eastern grocery stores. May be purchased frozen or from the dairy case of some supermarkets and gourmet food stores.

Fool, ful or foul *(Arabic):* see fava beans.

Garbanzo-Bean flour, ard-e nokhod-chi *(Persian):* a high-protein flour used in ground-meat mixtures and other dishes in place of flour. Each cup of garbanzo-bean flour is equivalent to 1/4 cup all-purpose flour.

Garbanzo beans, hummus *(Arabic):* small tan-colored beans. Dried beans are cooked and used to make dips or falafel. Lima beans may be substituted. Garbanzo-bean mix for making Hummus bi-Tahini, a dip, is available in packaged form.

Grape Leaves: leaves of grape vines, parboiled or preserved to use as wrappers for various stuffings. See Preserved Grape Leaves, page 136.

Halva *(Turkish);* **halwa** *(Persian, Arabic):* a pudding-like sweet made with flour, semolina, cornstarch or farina. Widely used in Middle Eastern cooking.

Harissa, heriseh *(Arabic):* a hot paste used as a condiment or dipping sauce in North African, Jordanian, Palestinian and Israeli cooking.

Hummus *(Arabic):* see garbanzo beans.

Kasseri *(Greek):* a firm, cream-colored cheese made from goat's milk or sheep's milk. Used as a table cheese or for frying. Provolone, Bulgarian kashkaval or Turkish kaser may be substituted.

Kaymak *(Turkish):* a clotted cream equivalent to English Devonshire cream or French crème fraîche. Used as a topping on sweet pastries. Devonshire cream, crème fraîche or whipped cream may be substituted. See Clotted Cream, page 131.

Kefalotiri *(Greek):* a hard cheese used chiefly for grating. Substitute Romano or Parmesan.

Khubz Arabi *(Arabic):* see arabic pocket bread or pita.

Laban *(Arabic):* see yogurt.

Lavash *(Armenian, Persian)*: circular cracker bread. See Cracker Bread, page 46.

Mahlab *(Arabic)*; **mahlepi** *(Greek)*: ground kernels of cherry stones. Usually sold whole but may be ground to order. Used as a flavoring for pastries, cakes and cookies in Arabic and Greek cuisines.

Mast *(Persian)*: see yogurt.

Mastic; mastik *(Middle East)*; **mastiche** *(Greek)*: a resin from a Mediterranean evergreen tree, Pistacia lentiscus, used in making chewing gum, incense, varnish, and flavoring pastries and liquor.

Mlookhiyah *(Arabic)*: a plant from the jute family. Arabs use the leaves to make a gelatinous soup. In Egypt, the leaves are chopped, cooked with seasonings and served over rice. Leaves may be dried or fresh.

Orange-Blossom Water: a distilled liquid from orange blossoms. Used to flavor pastries, creams and syrups.

Orzo *(Italian)*; **kridaraki** *(Greek)*; **rosemarina** *(American)*: small rice-shaped noodles used in soups and meat dishes in Greek and Mediterranean cooking.

Ouzo *(Greek)*; **raki** *(Turkish)*; **arak** *(Arabic)*: a colorless, anise-seed-flavored cordial that becomes milky when water is added. Whiskey may be substituted.

Pita, pide *(Turkish)*; **pita** *(Greek)*; **khubz Arabi** *(Arabic)*: see Arabic pocket bread.

Raki *(Turkish)*: see arack or ouzo.

Retsina *(Greek)*: a white or red wine, flavored with pine resin.

Rose Water: a solution of water and essence of roses. Used to flavor pastries and sweets in Arabic cooking; also used in making perfumes. Rose syrup and essence are available at gourmet grocery stores and are used by the drop when substituting for rose water.

Saffron, za'afaran *(Arabic)*: dried yellow stigmas of the purplish flower of the crocus family. Used as a seasoning, especially in stews and curries. Available at supermarkets but very expensive. Mexican varieties are less costly, but not as aromatic. Turmeric is sometimes substituted.

Sarma *(Turkish)*: see dolma.

Semolina: the heart of durum wheat, processed to make pasta products and couscous. Grains vary from very fine meal to pellets. The meal is used in pastries. See couscous. Sometimes rice or wheat farina may be substituted.

Sesame-Seed Paste, tahini paste *(Arabic)*: an oily paste made from ground sesame seeds. Used to make dips and sauces.

Sesame-Seed Sauce: see tahini.

Sumac *(Arabic)*: ground seeds of a non-poisonous plant of the cashew family used as a seasoning. (Not to be confused with the poisonous plants of the cashew family, such as poison ivy.) Use only the seeds sold at Middle Eastern and gourmet grocery stores.

Syrian Cheese: also known as *mountain cheese*. Resembles Monterey Jack cheese or Munster in texture and flavor. They may be used interchangeably.

Tahini *(Arabic)*: the sauce made from sesame-seed paste. Also refers to the oily paste sold in cans or jars at Middle Eastern grocery stores. See Sesame-Seed Sauce, page 41.

Tarama *(Greek)*: red or white roe of carp. Eaten plain or used to make dips.

Taramosalata *(Greek)*: dip made from red or white roe of carp (tarama).

Za'tar *(Arabic)*: a blend of spices including thyme, marjoram, sumac and salt.

APPETIZERS

If there is a meal course that best illuminates the spirit of Middle Eastern hospitality, it is the *meze* or *maza*, the Arabic pronunciation for the word appetizer.

Each country enjoys a unique style of dining over meze. Iranians begin the meal with a plate of mixed herbs, including coriander, parsley or mint with white cheese and a dip of yogurt mixed with cucumber called *Mast-o Khiar*. This is served with squares of chewy Persian Flat Bread known as *Nan-e Barbari*.

Lebanese and Syrians often enjoy elaborate meze tables with as many as 40 hot and cold Arab and Turkish-style dishes arriving simultaneously or in a glorious procession.

The Gulf States Arabic maza can be a simple bowl of nuts, some cooked fava beans, a few herbs, such as mint or parsley, or crisp romaine leaves or green onions.

Turkish meze tables are a feast of hot and cold dishes arriving on tiny plates, their contents depending on the chef's whim. The chef at Abudullah restaurant on the Bosphorus dazzled us with an ongoing array of appetizers, including sauced meat balls, pickles, marinated beans and liver brochettes among dozens more.

In Morocco, we experienced numerous styles of meze from French-style delicacies served at a coffee table before dinner to a

MENU

Thousand Nights Cocktail Party

Feta Cheese, Green and Black Olives, Green Onions

Eggplant Dip, page 24

Fish Roe Dip, page 22

Garbanzo-Bean Balls, pages 23, 24

Chilled Celery, Cucumbers and Radishes

Yogurt Sauce, page 40

Sesame-Seed Sauce, page 41

Miniature Arabic Pocket Bread, page 50

bowlful of honey and bread in a remote mountain village.

Greek appetizers may be as simple as a plate of cheese and olives or as exotic as fish-roe dips.

Beverages

Arabs from Saudi Arabia crossed the Red Sea and discovered coffee in East Africa. Its reputation grew as a pleasurable brew that kept sleepy Islamic priests awake during their devotions. Today coffee is enjoyed with many of the same ceremonial gestures and marks of etiquette as it was centuries ago.

Most Middle Easterners make a strong, thick brew from roasted coffee beans that have been pulverized and boiled in a long-handled pot called a *jezveh*. Flavor preferences differ from place to place. Arabs enjoy coffee flavored with cardamom, while Yemenites add ginger and Tunisians stir in rose water.

Tea, like coffee, undoubtedly was first used medicinally and attributed with healing powers. The Chinese emperor Shen Nung is credited with the discovery of tea in 2737 BC. Tea was probably traded between India and China for centuries before traveling with spice caravans to the Middle East and the West.

A dark brew—generally a mixture of Ceylonese and English blends—is preferred in Iraq, and many other Middle Eastern countries, including Turkey. Tea is served in tiny jigger-like glasses with or without cradles and saucers.

In Morocco every family—rich or poor—owns a tea service whether made of brass, silver or pewter. When it is served at breakfast, lunch, dinner and snacks, the family elder presides. Only the practiced elder knows the precise moment the tea is at perfection.

Almost every cuisine boasts a favorite yogurt drink, whether flavored with garlic as in Turkey or with mint as in Iran. Lebanese sometimes add sugar to taste.

Meat-Stuffed Grape Leaves
Dolmades (Greece)

Greek cooks sometimes line the saucepan with lamb ribs or bones to form a rack for the stuffed grape leaves. Rhubarb stalks are sometimes used as a rack to add interesting flavor.

1/4 cup olive oil
1 medium onion, minced
1 lb. ground lean lamb or beef
1/2 cup short-grain rice
2 tablespoons chopped fresh mint or 2 teaspoons crushed dried-leaf mint
2 tablespoons chopped fresh dill or 2 teaspoons dill weed

Salt and freshly ground pepper to taste
3/4 cup water
Juice of 1/2 lemon (1-1/2 tablespoons)
50 to 60 Preserved Grape Leaves, page 136
2 lemons, thinly sliced
Boiling water
Lemon juice to taste

Heat olive oil in a large skillet. Add onion. Sauté until onion is tender. Add meat. Cook until meat is crumbly and browned. Add rice, mint, dill, salt and pepper. Stir over medium heat until rice is glazed. Add 3/4 cup water. Bring to a simmer. Cook, uncovered, over medium heat 5 minutes or until liquid is absorbed. Stir in juice of 1/2 lemon. Cool. Cut stems from grape leaves. Place grape leaves in a large bowl. Pour boiling water over leaves. Drain and rinse. Cool. Line bottom of a large saucepan with 2 or 3 large leaves. Place each leaf shiny-side down on a flat surface. Spoon about 1 tablespoon meat mixture in center of each leaf. Roll up, tucking in ends as you roll. Stack rolls seam-side down in an even layer over grape leaves in saucepan. Arrange 2 or 3 lemon slices over rolls. Repeat layering rolls and lemon slices. Invert a heatproof plate on top of stuffed leaves while cooking. Press plate down gently.

Pour in water to within 1 inch of saucepan rim. Cover and simmer over low heat 40 minutes or until rice is tender. Leaves should be tender but chewy. Cool slightly. Arrange on a platter. Sprinkle with lemon juice to taste. Makes 50 to 60 appetizers.

Eggplant-Sesame Dip
Baba Ghannouj (Arabic)

An enticing dip for Arabic bread or a distinctive topping for hamburgers.

1 large eggplant
1/2 cup sesame-seed paste
*   (tahini paste)*
2 tablespoons vegetable oil
Juice of 2 lemons (6 tablespoons)

2 garlic cloves, cut in halves
Salt and freshly ground white
*   pepper to taste*
Chopped parsley or pomegranate
*   seeds, if desired*

Preheat oven to 400F (205C). Use a fork to pierce eggplant in several places. Place pierced eggplant on oven rack and bake 1 hour or until soft. If using microwave oven, bake pierced eggplant at full power (HIGH) 5 minutes or until soft. Cool. Peel. Dice pulp into a blender or food processor. Add sesame-seed paste, oil, lemon juice, garlic, salt and pepper. Process until mixture is smooth and pale. Spoon into a serving bowl. Garnish with parsley or pomegranate seeds, if desired. Makes 2 cups.

Garbanzo-Bean Dip
Hummus bi-Tahini (Arabic)

Scoop up this mellow dip with pieces of Arabic pocket bread or raw-vegetable dippers.

1 (1-lb.) can garbanzo beans, drained	Juice of 1 lemon (3 tablespoons)
2 tablespoons sesame-seed paste (tahini paste)	Salt and freshly ground pepper to taste
2 garlic cloves, minced	1 tablespoon vegetable oil
	1 or 2 parsley sprigs

Place garbanzo beans in blender or food processor. Process until smooth. Add sesame-seed paste, garlic, lemon juice, salt and pepper. Stir to blend. Shape mixture into a mound on a flat plate. Press your finger in center of mound to make an indentation. Fill indentation with oil. Garnish with parsley sprigs. Makes about 1 cup.

Fish-Roe Dip
Taramosalata (Greece)

Serve this snappy dip with crackers or spread it on toast.

1/3 (8-oz.) jar carp roe	4 slices firm white bread
1 small onion, grated	Water
1 garlic clove, cut	2 tablespoons red-wine vinegar or lemon juice
1 cup olive oil	

In blender, combine roe, onion, garlic and 2 tablespoons olive oil. Blend until smooth. Place bread in water to cover. Lift bread from water and squeeze dry. Bread should have the consistency of wet cotton. Add to roe mixture in blender alternately with remaining olive oil and vinegar or lemon juice. Blend until thickened and smooth. Cover and refrigerate to chill. Makes about 1-1/2 cups.

Middle Eastern Pizza
Lahmajun (Armenia)

You'll like this easy version—it uses frozen dough.

1 lb. ground lean beef or lamb	2 tablespoons sugar
3 tablespoons tomato sauce	1 tablespoon toasted pine nuts,
3 tablespoons grenadine syrup	page 46
1 teaspoon salt	1 (1-lb.) loaf frozen bread dough,
1/4 cup minced onion	thawed

Preheat oven to 350F (175C). Lightly grease baking sheets. In a large bowl, combine meat, tomato sauce, grenadine syrup, salt, onion, sugar and pine nuts. Mix well; set aside. Divide dough into 6 equal portions. On a lightly floured surface, roll each portion into a 4-inch circle. Place on prepared baking sheets. Divide meat mixture into 6 equal portions. Place 1 portion on each dough circle. Spread to within 1/2 inch of edge of dough. Bake 20 to 25 minutes or until golden. Makes 6 pizzas.

Garbanzo-Bean Balls
Falafel (Arabic)

A popular street food since ancient times.

1 cup dried garbanzo beans, sorted, rinsed	1 teaspoon ground cumin
	1/2 teaspoon baking soda
Water	Salt and freshly ground pepper
3 green onions	to taste
1/2 cup packed parsley sprigs	Oil for frying
4 garlic cloves	Sesame seeds, if desired
1 egg	

Soak beans in water to cover overnight. Drain. Place beans in food mill or processor. Add green onions, parsley, garlic, egg, cumin, baking soda, salt and pepper. Process until almost smooth. Let stand 15 minutes. Refrigerate to chill. Pour oil 1 inch deep into a large skillet. Heat to 370F (190C) on a deep-fry thermometer. Moisten your hands and pinch off pieces of bean mixture 3/4 inch in diameter. Shape into small balls with your hands, or use a wet melon-ball scoop. If patties are desired, use 1 tablespoon bean mixture for each 2-inch patty. Roll in sesame seeds, if desired. Fry in hot oil until browned on all sides, about 2 minutes. Serve with wooden picks. Makes about 24 balls or 12 patties.

Fill Arabic pocket-bread halves with Garbanzo-Bean Patties. Add shredded lettuce, diced tomato, pickles, sliced radishes, olives and green onions. Drizzle with Sesame-See Sauce, page 41. A dab of harissa or Hot Sauce, page 42, is a must.

Variation
✳ Substitute 1 (1-pound) can garbanzo beans, drained, for soaked dried garbanzo beans.

Eggplant Dip
Melintzanosalata (Greece)

Easy eggplant dip can be served as a salad. It's similar to Italian caponata.

1 large eggplant
2 medium tomatoes, chopped
2 tablespoons chopped fresh
   parsley
1 small onion, grated
2 garlic cloves, minced

1/2 cup olive oil
2 tablespoons red-wine vinegar
   or lemon juice
Salt and freshly ground pepper
   to taste

Preheat oven to 400F (205C). Use a fork to pierce eggplant in several places. Place pierced eggplant on oven rack and bake 1 hour or until soft. If using microwave oven, bake pierced eggplant at full power (HIGH) 5 minutes or until soft. Cool. Peel and chop. Place chopped eggplant in a large salad bowl. Add remaining ingredients. Mix well. Refrigerate to chill. Makes 6 to 8 servings.

Feta Cheese Dip

Beyaz Peynir Ezmesi (Turkey)

The recipe calls for feta cheese, but pot, hoop or dry-curd cottage cheese also may be used.

1 cup crumbled feta cheese
2 tablespoons olive oil

1/4 cup chopped parsley
1/4 cup chopped dill

Combine cheese, half the olive oil and half each of the parsley and dill in blender container. Whir until blended. Add remaining oil, parsley and dill and blend until smooth. Serve as cold dip for cut raw vegetables. Makes about 1 cup.

Mixed-Herb Plate

Sabzi Khordan (Iran)

Fragrant fresh herbs are ideal as appetizers or in place of a salad with the meal.

Mint sprigs
Green onions
Fresh Italian parsley (flat-leaf)
Watercress sprigs
1/2 lb. feta cheese, cut into
cubes, if desired

Cherry tomatoes or small
tomatoes, cut into wedges,
if desired
Cucumber-Yogurt Sauce,
opposite, if desired

Arrange mint, green onions, parsley and watercress on a platter. Place cheese cubes and cherry or cut tomatoes on platter, if desired. Serve with Cucumber-Yogurt Sauce, if desired. Makes 6 servings.

Cucumber-Yogurt Sauce
Mast-o Khiar (Iran)

The versatile sauce is wonderful with fresh raw vegetables.

2 cucumbers, peeled, thinly
    sliced
2 tablespoons chopped green
    onion
2 cups plain yogurt
Salt and freshly ground white
    pepper to taste

1 tablespoon crushed dried-leaf
    mint
1/2 cup raisins, if desired
1/4 cup chopped walnuts, if
    desired

    Combine cucumber and green onion. Stir in yogurt, salt, pepper and mint. Add raisins and walnuts, if desired. Cover and refrigerate until ready to use. Makes 4 cups.

SOUPS, SALADS & SAUCES

Soups

Of the many categories of soup, bean soup is a mainstay in many Mideast-Mediterranean cuisines.

In Greece and Turkey, bean soups are usually given a final touch of lemon juice or vinegar and a light drizzle of oil. Here also you will find several delicate and elegant versions of Egg & Lemon Soup. No wedding or special event is complete without one of these soups.

If beans are basic, lentils run a close second. Moroccan Soup, or Harira, the national soup of Morocco, is a fine example of how artful soup made with lentils can be.

Iranian soups created by ancient Persians are by far the most complex. Who else would think of combining lentils with pomegranates?

Yogurt soups are another major soup category. Each region—indeed each cook—boasts a favorite recipe. Some yogurt soups, generally with a chicken or meat base, are served hot, while others are served cold as a summer refreshment before or after a meal.

Salads

In the Middle East salads are usually served as appetizers because they are a natural addition to the meze table.

Exciting and colorful salads of North Africa are actually accompaniments for couscous dishes. They are usually served in clusters, but stand well on their own.

Yogurt salads are common to all Middle Eastern cuisines. They can be refreshing summertime appetizers or wonderful condiments to go with fish.

Salads made with grains or beans, such as taboulleh made with cracked wheat and parsley, and marinated bean salads are commonly served in the Arab world. They make practical choices for long-standing buffets because they can be made ahead and, once placed on the table, require no rearranging or recrisping.

No table in Greece or Turkey is without a tossed green salad to help balance the main meal. In Istanbul, a street meal of lamb kebabs includes a shepherd's salad made with sliced cucumber, onion and tomatoes, dressed simply at the table with oil and vinegar to taste.

Sauces

Every cuisine has flavor superstars and in the Middle East, sesame seeds, garlic, yogurt and lemon seem to dominate the scene.

The most-adored sauce in the Arab world is sesame-seed sauce, generally known as *tahini*. The sauce is made from seeds ground to an oily paste. It is used to flavor foods or added to pureed vegetables, such as eggplant or garbanzo beans. Sesame-seed sauce may be diluted to spoon over fish, meat, vegetables or salads. Pocket-bread sandwiches are rarely without a smidgen of tahini. Tahini is also used extensively in sweets.

Garlic, dill and mint are favorite ingredients in yogurt sauces. Egg and lemon is a favorite flavor duo in Greece. Mixing egg and lemon into hot liquid is such a delicate process that even veteran cooks may say a few words of prayer to ward off curdling. The best method to avoid curdling is to mix a small amount of the hot liquid into the egg-and-lemon mixture in a small bowl before adding it to the bulk of the hot liquid. Cooking the sauce over too-high heat or cooking it too long will cause curdling.

Oil-and-lemon dressing is another dominant sauce in Mideast-Mediterranean cooking. Most cooks add oil and lemon juice to both vegetables and salads by eye and feel, rarely by measure. Vinegar is frequently substituted for lemon juice. Every salad has individual requirements which no scientific measuring system can satisfy.

MENU

Tunisian Couscous Supper

Almonds

Moroccan Olives

Tunisian Couscous, page 66

Carrot & Orange Salad page 36

Mixed Salad page 37

Zucchini Relish Salad page 36

French Cigarettes, page 124

Minted Tea

Chicken Broth

A basic chicken broth to use in recipes throughout this book.

2 lbs. chicken necks, backs or gizzards	*1 large onion, quartered*
8 cups water (2 qts.)	*Few parsley sprigs*
2 celery stalks with leaves	*2 bay leaves*
2 small carrots	*Salt to taste*
1 small parsnip, quartered	*6 whole peppercorns*
	Few dill sprigs, if desired

Combine all ingredients in a large saucepan. Bring to a boil. Reduce heat and cover. Simmer over low heat 2 to 2-1/2 hours. Cool uncovered. Strain. Reserve meat and vegetables for use in other soups or sauces. Pour into a clean jar or jars. Use immediately or cover and refrigerate up to 2 days. Broth may be frozen in freezer containers with lids, leaving 1 inch headspace. Makes 1 quart.

Beef Broth

Use this basic recipe whenever a recipe calls for beef broth.

3 lbs. beef bones with meat or chuck beef with bones	*2 small carrots*
8 cups water (2 qts.)	*2 bay leaves*
1 medium onion, quartered	*Few parsley sprigs*
1 garlic clove	*Salt to taste*
2 celery stalks with leaves	*6 whole peppercorns*

Combine all ingredients in a large saucepan. Bring to a boil. Reduce heat and cover. Simmer over low heat 2 to 2-1/2 hours. Cool uncovered. Strain. Reserve meat and vegetables for use in other soups or sauces. Pour into a clean jar or jars. Use immediately or cover and refrigerate up to 2 days. Broth may be frozen in freezer containers with lids, leaving 1 inch headspace. Makes 1 quart.

Bulgur & Yogurt Soup
Tanabur (Armenia)

Yogurt and bulgur make this soup especially wholesome.

1/2 cup fine- to medium-grade
   bulgur
Water
6 cups Beef Broth (1-1/2 qts.),
   page 29
3 cups plain yogurt
1 egg, beaten

Salt and freshly ground white
   pepper to taste
2 tablespoons butter or
   margarine
1 small onion, minced
1/4 cup chopped fresh mint or
   1 tablespoon crushed dried-
   leaf mint

Place bulgur in a medium bowl. Cover with water. Soak until water is absorbed, about 1 hour. Squeeze dry. Pour broth into a large saucepan. Bring to a boil. Add softened bulgur. Stir to mix well. Simmer, uncovered, over low heat until bulgur is tender, about 30 minutes. Beat yogurt, egg, salt and pepper in a medium bowl. Gradually stir into bulgur mixture. Reduce heat to very low to prevent yogurt from separating. Melt butter or margarine in a small skillet. Add onion. Sauté until onion is tender. Add mint. Sauté 1 minute. Stir into soup just before serving. Makes 8 servings.

Moroccan Soup
Harira (Morocco)

Morocco's national soup is eaten for breakfast, lunch or dinner.

*8 cups Beef Broth (2 qts.),
  page 29
1/2 lb. boneless lamb, diced
1 large carrot, cut up
Salt and freshly ground pepper
  to taste
1 (1-lb.) can whole tomatoes,
  drained
1 cup lentils, sorted, rinsed
1/2 teaspoon saffron threads or
  powder*

*4 small onions, quartered
1 cup chopped cilantro
1 cup chopped fresh parsley
Juice of 1 lemon (3 tablespoons)
2 tablespoons butter or
  margarine
1/4 cup all-purpose flour
Freshly ground pepper
Chopped parsley for garnish*

Combine broth, lamb, carrot, salt and pepper in a large saucepan. Bring to a boil. Reduce heat and cover. Simmer over low heat 1 hour. Crush tomatoes with the back of a spoon. Add lentils, saffron, onions and crushed tomatoes to soup. Simmer, covered, over low heat 40 minutes or until lentils are tender. Add cilantro, 1 cup parsley and lemon juice. Knead butter or margarine into flour to make a ball. Add to soup. Stir occasionally over medium heat until flour ball melts, about 5 minutes. Sprinkle with additional pepper and parsley. Makes 6 to 8 servings.

☀ Egg & Lemon Soup
Avgolemono Soupa (Greece)

Orzo, the noodle that looks like rice, is available at most Middle Eastern grocery stores.

10 cups Chicken Broth
   (2-1/2 qts.), page 29
1 small onion, halved
4 garlic cloves, crushed
2 celery stalks with leaves
3 parsley sprigs
1 carrot, quartered
2 bay leaves

Giblets from 1 chicken, if desired
2/3 cup orzo
Salt and freshly ground pepper
   to taste
4 eggs
Juice of 2 lemons (6 tablespoons)
Additional freshly ground
   pepper

Combine broth, onion, garlic, celery, parsley, carrot and bay leaves in a large saucepan. Add giblets, if desired. Bring to a boil. Reduce heat and cover. Simmer over low heat 20 minutes or until giblets are tender. If not using giblets, just bring to a boil. Strain broth into a bowl. Return broth to saucepan and discard vegetables. Add orzo, salt and pepper to broth. Bring to a boil. Reduce heat and cover. Simmer over low heat 15 to 20 minutes or until orzo is soft. Place eggs and lemon juice in blender. Process until smooth. Add about 1 cup soup to egg mixture in blender. Blend until frothy. Add another 1 cup soup to mixture in blender. Process to blend. Add to soup in saucepan. If desired, dice giblets and add to soup. Stir constantly over low heat to bring to serving temperature. Do not boil or mixture will curdle. Sprinkle with additional pepper. Makes 6 to 8 servings.

Variations
✱ Chilled Egg & Lemon Soup: Process cooked soup in blender until smooth. Refrigerate to chill. When ready to serve, beat 1 cup whipping cream until soft peaks form. Fold thoroughly into soup. Sprinkle with freshly ground pepper. Garnish with lemon slices.

卍卍卍卍卍卍卍卍卍卍卍卍卍卍卍卍卍卍卍卍卍卍卍卍卍卍卍卍卍

☀ Chilled Cucumber-Yogurt Soup
Tsatsaki (Greece)

Begin or end a meal with this refreshing summer soup.

*2 large cucumbers, peeled,
coarsely shredded
2 garlic cloves, crushed
1 tablespoon chopped fresh mint
or 1 teaspoon crushed dried-
leaf mint*

*2 cups plain yogurt
2 cups buttermilk
Salt to taste
1 tablespoon olive oil, if desired
1 tablespoon vinegar, if desired*

Combine cucumber, garlic, mint and yogurt in a large bowl. Stir gently to mix well. Stir in buttermilk and salt. Sprinkle with oil and vinegar, if desired. Makes 6 to 8 servings.

Variations
✳ Arabic Cucumber-Yogurt Soup *(Khyar bi-Laban)*: Omit oil and vinegar.
✳ Israeli Cucumber-Yogurt Soup *(Tarato)*: Omit mint. Top soup with 2 or 3 tablespoons chopped almonds.
✳ Persian Cucumber-Yogurt Soup *(Dugh Khiar)*: Omit oil and vinegar. Add 1 tablespoon chopped green onion and 1/4 cup raisins to yogurt mixture.
✳ Turkish Cucumber-Yogurt Soup *(Cacik)*: Add 1 teaspoon dill weed or 1 tablespoon minced fresh dill.

Bean Soup

Fasoulada (Greece)

A bit of olive oil and lemon juice adds a final touch.

2 tablespoons olive oil
2 medium onions, thinly sliced
2 tablespoons tomato paste
1 large carrot, thinly sliced
1 large celery stalk, sliced
2 tablespoons chopped fresh
   parsley (flat-leaf)
1 teaspoon dill weed or
   1 tablespoon minced fresh
   dill leaf

8 cups water (2 qts.)
1 lb. Great Northern beans
Salt and freshly ground pepper
   to taste
1 tablespoon olive oil, if desired
2 tablespoons lemon juice or
   vinegar, if desired

Heat 2 tablespoons olive oil in a large saucepan. Add onions. Sauté until tender. Stir in tomato paste. Cook 1 minute to blend flavors. Add carrot, celery, parsley and dill weed or dill leaf. Cook and stir until carrots are glazed, about 5 minutes. Add water, beans, salt and pepper. Bring to a boil. Reduce heat and cover. Simmer over low heat 1 hour or longer until beans are tender. Sprinkle 1 tablespoon olive oil, lemon juice or vinegar over soup before serving or serve separately. Makes 8 to 10 servings.

Variation
✳ Bean Soup with Meat: Sauté 2 pounds short ribs or beef or 1 pound chuck beef, cubed, in olive oil until browned on all sides. Add onions. Continue with recipe, cooking soup 1-1/2 to 2 hours or until beef is tender.

Pomegranate-Lentil Soup
Ash-e Anar (Iran)

If using fresh pomegranates, extract the juice with an orange juicer.

3/4 cup lentils
2 tablespoons butter or
    margarine
1 medium onion, chopped
8 cups water (2 qts.)
1 cup long-grain rice
1 teaspoon turmeric
Salt and freshly ground pepper
    to taste
1/2 cup chopped fresh parsley

1/2 cup chopped green onions
1 cup pomegranate juice or
    1/4 cup grenadine syrup
1 tablespoon butter or
    margarine
2 tablespoons chopped fresh
    mint or 2 teaspoons crushed
    dried-leaf mint
1 tablespoons raisins

Rinse lentils several times. Set aside to drain. Melt 2 tablespoons butter or margarine in a large saucepan. Add onion. Sauté until onion is tender. Add water, drained lentils, rice, turmeric, salt and pepper. Bring to a boil. Reduce heat and cover. Simmer over low heat 40 minutes or until lentils and rice are tender. Add parsley, green onions and pomegranate juice or grenadine syrup. Simmer 15 minutes or longer. Melt 1 tablespoon butter or margarine in a small skillet. Add mint. Sauté until butter or margarine is golden brown. Pour over soup. Sprinkle with raisins. Makes 6 to 8 servings.

Carrot & Orange Salad
Salatat Jazar w'Lamoon (Morocco)

This fragrant salad is often served with a couscous dish in Morocco.

1 lb. carrots, grated
Juice of 1 lemon (3 tablespoons)
1 tablespoon orange-blossom
   water

1/8 teaspoon sugar
Pinch of salt
2 oranges, peeled, sliced
Parsley sprigs, if desired

In a medium salad bowl, combine carrots, lemon juice, orange-blossom water, sugar and salt. Toss to mix well. Arrange orange slices around mixture. Garnish with parsley, if desired. Makes 6 servings.

Zucchini-Relish Salad
Ajlouk (Tunisia)

One of the satellite salads for Tunisian Couscous, page 66, also makes a tasty dip.

2 medium zucchini
1 cup water
Juice of 1/2 lemon
   (1-1/2 tablespoons)

1 garlic clove, minced
Dash of hot-pepper sauce
1/2 teaspoon caraway seeds

Place zucchini in a large skillet. Add water. Bring to a boil. Reduce heat and cover. Simmer over low heat 15 minutes or until zucchini is soft. Drain. Place zucchini in a medium bowl. Coarsely mash with a fork. Add remaining ingredients. Mix well. Refrigerate to chill. Makes 6 relish servings.

Mixed Salad
Slata Jidda (Tunisia)

Serve in a small bowl as an accompaniment for Tunisian Couscous, page 66.

1 tomato, chopped
1/2 medium, green pepper, diced
1 small cucumber, peeled, diced
2 green onions, minced

1 garlic clove, minced
2 tablespoons lemon juice
Salt to taste

Combine all ingredients in a medium bowl. Toss to mix well. Refrigerate to chill. Makes 6 relish servings or 2 large servings.

Parsley-Wheat Salad
Taboulleh (Lebanon/Syria)

Make this traditional salad in the morning and it will be ready in time for dinner.

2 cups fine- to medium-grade
    bulgur
Water
3 cups finely chopped fresh
    parsley (about 6 bunches)
1/4 cup chopped fresh mint or
    2 tablespoons crushed dried-
    leaf mint
1 tablespoon minced fresh dill or
    1 teaspoon dill weed
1 cup chopped green onions
4 medium tomatoes, diced

1 medium cucumber, peeled,
    chopped
1 cup olive oil
1 cup lemon juice
Salt and freshly ground pepper
    to taste
Romaine lettuce leaves
Black Marinated Greek Olives,
    page 138, for garnish
Tomato wedges and mint sprigs
    for garnish

Place bulgur in a large bowl. Add water to cover and let stand about 1 hour or until bulgur doubles in size and most of the liquid is absorbed. Drain well and squeeze dry. Add parsley, mint, dill, green onions, tomatoes and cucumber. Toss gently. Add olive oil, lemon juice, salt and pepper. Toss to mix well. Refrigerate. To serve, line a salad bowl with lettuce leaves. Mound salad on lettuce leaves. Garnish with olives, tomato wedges and mint. Makes 12 servings.

Pocket-Bread Salad
Fattoush (Arabic)

Triangles of toasted pocket bread give distinction to a tossed salad.

2 (4-inch) or 1 (8-inch) Arabic pocket bread
8 hearts of romaine lettuce
1 medium cucumber, diced
2 large tomatoes, diced
4 green onions, sliced
1/4 cup chopped fresh parsley
1/2 cup chopped fresh mint or 1 tablespoon crushed dried-leaf mint

1/2 cup chopped watercress, if desired
1/2 cup olive oil
1/2 cup lemon juice (5 or 6 lemons)
1 garlic clove, minced
Salt and freshly ground pepper to taste

Place pocket bread on broiler rack 4 inches from heat source. Broil until toasted. Turn and toast other side. Toast should be very crisp but not charred. Break into bite-size pieces or cut into triangles. Place in a large salad bowl. Break lettuce into bowl. Add cucumber, tomatoes, onions, parsley and mint. Add watercress, if desired. Toss. Combine remaining ingredients in a small bowl or jar. Stir or shake to mix well. Pour over salad. Toss to mix well. Serve immediately. Makes 6 servings.

Greek Village Salad
Choriatiki Salata (Greece)

Almost any vegetable may be added to this beautiful mixed salad.

4 or 5 medium tomatoes, cut in wedges
1 medium cucumber, sliced diagonally
1 small green pepper, thinly sliced
5 green onions, sliced
5 radishes, sliced
1/2 small head romaine lettuce
2 tablespoons chopped fresh dill or 2 teaspoons dill weed
15 green or black Marinated Greek Olives, page 138

Salt and freshly ground black pepper to taste
1/4 cup olive oil
1/4 cup vinegar
1 large garlic clove, minced
2 tablespoons chopped fresh parsley
Pinch of crushed dried-leaf oregano
1/4 lb. feta cheese, diced (about 1/2 cup)

Combine tomatoes, cucumber, green pepper, green onions, radishes, lettuce, dill and olives in a large, shallow salad bowl. Add salt and black pepper. Toss to mix well. Combine remaining ingredients except cheese in a small bowl or jar. Stir or shake to mix well. Pour over salad. Toss gently but thoroughly. Garnish with feta cheese. Makes 6 to 8 servings.

Score and cube feta cheese by cutting with a string.

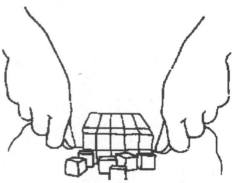

Egg & Lemon Sauce

Avgolemono (Greece)

A special flavoring for chicken soup or a topping for meatballs, savory pastry, fish or vegetables.

Juice of 2 lemons (6 tablespoons)
2 eggs or egg yolks
1 cup hot Chicken Broth,
*   page 29*

Salt and freshly ground pepper
*   to taste*

To blend Egg & Lemon Sauce into hot soup, beat a small amount of hot soup into sauce. Pour sauce into remaining hot soup. Reheat over low heat. If heat is too high, sauce will curdle.

Combine lemon juice and eggs or egg yolks in blender. With blender still running, gradually add hot broth. Add salt and pepper. Process until frothy. Makes about 2 cups.

Yogurt Sauce

Laban (Arabic)

Basic sauce tops everything—meats, fish, poultry, pasta, rice, vegetables and even sandwiches.

2 garlic cloves, crushed
Salt and freshly ground white
*   pepper to taste*

1 cup plain yogurt

Combine all ingredients in a small bowl. Mix well. Refrigerate to chill. Makes 1 cup.

Variations
* Mint-Yogurt Sauce: Add 1 teaspoon crushed dried-leaf mint.
* Tomato-Yogurt Sauce: Add 1 tablespoon tomato puree or

1 teaspoon tomato paste. Serve on seafood salads.
❋ Yogurt Dressing: Add 1 teaspoon vegetable oil and 1 teaspoon
lemon juice or vinegar. Serve as a topping on fried vegetables or as a
dressing in salads.

Sesame-Seed Sauce
Tahini (Arabic)

Prepared sesame-seed sauce, or tahini, is available from most
Middle Eastern food shops.

*1 cup sesame-seed paste (tahini
   paste)*
4 garlic cloves, minced
Juice of 2 lemons (6 tablespoons)
Salt to taste

About 1/2 cup water
*1 tablespoon chopped fresh
   parsley*
1 tablespoon olive oil, if desired

Combine sesame-seed paste, garlic, lemon juice and salt in blender.
Process until smooth. Gradually blend in water for desired
consistency. Mixture should be thick for a dip and thin for a topping.
Turn into a small bowl. Stir in parsley. For dips, press your finger in
center of dip, making an indentation. Fill indentation with olive oil. If
sauce is to be used as a topping, leave
plain. Makes 2 cups.

*Thick tahini is used as a dip or
coating. Thin tahini tops sandwiches,
salads, vegetables or fish.*

Turkish Salad
S'chug b'Ketchoff (Israel)

Created as a substitute for ketchup, this is actually a dressing for fillings in Arabic pocket bread.

1 (6-oz.) can tomato paste	1 cup chopped fresh parsley
1 tablespoon Hot Sauce, below, or harissa	1 medium tomato, finely chopped
1/4 teaspoon ground fenugreek	About 1/4 cup cold water

Place tomato paste in a medium bowl. Stir in Hot Sauce or harissa, fenugreek, parsley and tomato. Mix well. Thin with water to a smooth paste. Refrigerate to chill. Makes 1-1/2 cups.

Hot Sauce
Shug (Yemen)

A dipping sauce for bread and a seasoning for meats and sauces.

1 lb. hot yellow peppers	3 teaspoons freshly ground black pepper
1 garlic head, peeled	3 teaspoons ground cumin
2 teaspoons salt	

Remove stems from yellow peppers and discard. Place yellow peppers in food processor with garlic. Process until coarsely ground. Add remaining ingredients. Process until barely smooth. Makes about 2 cups.

Garlic Sauce
Skordalia (Greece)

Bread or potatoes give body to a versatile sauce that can be a dip or a topping for fish and vegetables.

4 garlic cloves
Juice of 2 lemons (6 tablespoons)
1/2 cup olive oil
Salt to taste

8 to 10 slices white bread,
*   crusts removed*
Water

In blender, combine garlic, lemon juice, olive oil and salt. Process until smooth. Soak bread in water and squeeze dry. Add moistened bread to garlic mixture. Process until smooth and creamy. Refrigerate sauce in a covered container. Use within 2 or 3 days. Makes about 2 cups.

Variations

✳ Garlic Sauce with Mashed Potato: Substitute 2 cups cold mashed potatoes for moistened bread. If sauce is too thick, add more water. Sauce will thicken when chilled.

✳ Garlic Sauce with Almonds: Add 1/4 cup ground unblanched almonds to mixture. Process until blended. If sauce is too thick, add more water.

BREADS

Arabic pocket bread, or *Khubz Arabi*, is probably the most inventive form of bread known. This ancient and incredibly versatile bread is known as *pita* in Greek, *peda* in Persian, *pide* in Turkish and *pocket bread* or *pita* in the United States. Its built-in pocket can be filled with vegetables, salads, meat, cheese or omelets to make a complete meal-in-hand. Or the bread can be used as a utensil for scooping up foods. The bread is soft enough to dunk into soup and sauces and hard enough to make chewing pleasurable. Many dishes use pocket bread as an edible basket for stews or as an edible tray for whole barbecued lambs. Crunchy, toasted Arab bread is often broken in pieces and tossed with herbs and vegetables to make a salad or to add to soups.

One of the most fascinating variations on the pocket-bread theme is the large Soft Bread Sheets called *nan-e lavash* by Persians, *tonir lavash* by Armenians, and *mar'ook* by Lebanese. This is the same bread East Indians call *tandoor* after the beehive-like oven on which it is baked. Shaped dough is slapped along the sides of the hot oven and removed by hand once cooked. An inverted wok works just as well. When baked until crisp, this bread becomes *lavash*, the large Cracker Bread, a delightful snack or a salad bread. Armenians also stack wet sheets of lavash between cheese for a breakfast snack, called *surrum*.

Pita bread is also the base for a category of pies known as *fatayer*. These pies are filled and formed into turnovers, triangles and open-face sandwiches.

Rather flat-ridged Persian breads are delightfully chewy. They are excellent with cheese, jam and

MENU
Morrocan Tent Supper

Chicken Pastry,
page 81

Moroccan Soup,
page 31

Moroccan Bread

Carrot & Orange Salad,
page 36

Minted Tea

butter for breakfast or for dunking into sauces. They tend to dry quickly, so wrap them carefully in plastic wrap as soon as they are out of the oven.

Moroccan Bread
Khubz (Morocco)

Moroccans use the crust of this delicious bread to scoop up saucy foods.

2-1/2 cups warm water (110F, 45C)	1 tablespoon salt
1 (1/4-oz.) pkg. active dry yeast (1 tablespoon)	About 6 cups all-purpose flour

Pour warm water into a large bowl. Sprinkle yeast over water. Stir until dissolved. Add salt. Gradually stir in about 6 cups flour until dough pulls away from side of bowl. Turn out onto a floured surface. Knead, adding more flour if necessary, until dough is smooth and elastic. Shape dough into a 12-inch roll. Cut roll into three 4-inch portions. Shape each portion into a ball, then into a dome-shaped loaf tapering from 1 inch high in center to 1/4 inch around edges. Place loaves on ungreased baking sheets

Cover with a dry cloth towel and let rise until doubled in bulk, about 1 hour. Preheat oven to 350F (175C). Make slashes in each loaf on 4 sides, crisscrossing at corners, if desired. Bake 20 to 30 minutes or until loaves are golden brown. Remove from baking sheets and cool on a rack. Serve warm or wrap cooled bread in plastic wrap and refrigerate. Bread may be stored for several days. Makes 3 loaves.

Cracker Bread
Lavash (Armenia)

Crisp matzo-like cracker bread is perfect with soups and salads.

1-1/2 cups warm water
   (110F, 45C)
 1 (1/4-oz.) pkg. active dry yeast
   (1 tablespoon)
 1 teaspoon salt
	2 cups all-purpose flour
	 About 2 cups whole-wheat flour
	 1/2 cup toasted sesame seeds,
	   below

Pour warm water into a large bowl. Sprinkle yeast over water. Stir until dissolved. Add salt. Combine all-purpose flour and 2 cups whole-wheat flour in a large bowl. Stir flour mixture into yeast mixture until dough pulls away from side of bowl. Turn out onto a floured surface. Knead, adding more whole-wheat flour if necessary, until dough is smooth and elastic. Shape into a ball. Place ball in a large greased bowl. Turn dough to grease all sides. Cover with a dry cloth towel. Let rise in a warm place until doubled in bulk, about 1-1/2 hours. Punch down and let rise again until doubled in bulk, about 30 minutes.

Preheat oven to 400F (205C). Lightly grease 2 baking sheets. Set aside. Pinch off a piece of dough about 2 inches in diameter. On a lightly floured surface, roll out each piece of dough to a paper-thin circle, about 9 inches in diameter. Place 1 or 2 on each baking sheet. Sprinkle each circle with 1 tablespoon sesame seeds. Bake 5 to 6 minutes or until bread is blistered and lightly browned. Place pale-side up under broiler a few seconds to brown lightly. Cool. Wrap in plastic wrap and store in a dry place. Makes 8 crackers.

To toast nuts and seeds: <u>Oven method</u>—Spread nuts or seeds in a single layer on a baking sheet. Toast in a preheated 375F (190C) oven, shaking pan occasionally, until nuts or seeds are golden. <u>Skillet method</u>—Spread nuts or seeds in a single layer in a skillet. Toast over low heat, shaking skillet frequently, until nuts or seeds are golden.

༺༻༺༻༺༻༺༻༺༻༺༻༺༻༺༻༺༻༺༻༺༻༺༻༺༻༺༻

☼ Persian Flat Bread

Nan-e Barbari (Iran)

Ridges in the bread are typically Iranian. Change the pattern as directed below for Armenian Peda Bread.

1/4 cup warm water (110F, 45C)	*3 tablespoons butter or*
1 (1/4-oz.) pkg. active dry yeast	* margarine, melted*
* (1 tablespoon)*	*2 cups warm water (110F, 45C)*
About 5 cups all-purpose flour	*Milk*
1-1/2 teaspoons salt	*1/4 cup sesame seeds*
3 tablespoons sugar	

Pour 1/4 cup warm water into a large bowl. Sprinkle yeast over water. Stir until dissolved. Place 5 cups flour in a large bowl. Make a well in center. Add yeast mixture, salt, sugar, butter or margarine and 2 cups warm water. Gradually stir flour into liquid mixture in well until dough is thoroughly mixed. Dough will be sticky. Turn out onto a floured surface. Knead, adding more flour if necessary, until dough is smooth and elastic. Place in a large greased bowl. Turn dough to grease all sides.

Cover with a dry cloth towel. Let stand until doubled in bulk, about 1 hour. Preheat oven to 350F (175C). Punch down dough. Divide into 4 equal portions. Shape each portion into a ball. Place on a floured surface and sprinkle with flour. Cover with a dry cloth towel. Let rest 20 minutes. Roll out each portion of dough to a 12" x 6" oval. Place on ungreased baking sheets. Use the side of your thumb to make ridges 1 inch apart lengthwise on each oval. Brush with milk. Sprinkle each oval with 1 tablespoon sesame seeds. Let rest 15 minutes. Bake 20 to 30 minutes or until golden brown. Remove from baking sheets and cool on racks. Serve warm or wrap cooled bread in plastic wrap and refrigerate. Makes 4 flat breads. (See next page for variations.)

Variations

✳ Armenian Peda Bread: After making ridges in dough, press with fingers all over surface of dough to make the traditional surface pattern. Continue with recipe.

✳ Batons: Cut each oval into 12" x 1/2" strips. Brush with milk and sprinkle with sesame seeds. Bake 15 minutes or until golden brown. Makes 12 batons.

✳ Bread Rings: Shape each ball into a log. Cut log into 4 equal pieces. Roll each piece into a 7-inch rope. Shape into a ring, pinching ends to seal. Place on baking sheets. Brush with milk and sprinkle with sesame seeds. Bake 15 minutes or until golden. Remove from baking sheets. Makes about 16 rings.

Greek Pita Bread
Pita (Greece)

Wrap this soft bread around a meat filling to make Souvlaki, opposite.

1 cup all-purpose flour
1 cup whole-wheat flour
1 teaspoon salt

About 1-1/4 cups water
Vegetable oil

In a large bowl, combine all-purpose flour, whole-wheat flour and salt. Mix well. Stir in just enough water to allow dough to pull away from side of bowl. If necessary, add a few drops of water to make dough pliable. Turn out onto a floured surface. Knead with your floured hands until dough is soft and smooth. Pinch off pieces of dough about 1-1/2 inches in diameter. Shape into balls. Cover with a dry cloth towel and let rest 10 minutes. Roll out to a circle about 6 inches in diameter. Heat griddle over medium-high heat. Lightly grease griddle with oil. Begin cooking when a drop of water sizzles on hot griddle. Cook each dough circle until browned underneath. Turn and brown other side. Bread will puff slightly when cooked. Serve warm or place immediately in plastic bags to keep soft. Makes 6 or 7 pita breads.

Greek Pita Sandwiches
Souvlaki (Greece)

A tavern in the Athens flea market served these delicious sandwiches with beer.

1 lb. ground beef or lamb
1 teaspoon crushed dried-leaf
   oregano
Salt and freshly ground pepper
   to taste
1 small onion
2 cups shredded cabbage

1 large tomato, chopped
2 tablespoons lemon juice
2 tablespoons olive oil
Salt to taste
6 Greek Pita Breads, opposite,
   or small flour tortillas
Paprika

Combine ground meat, oregano, salt and pepper to taste in a medium bowl. Mix thoroughly. Pinch off pieces of mixture about 1 inch in diameter. Form into small sausage shapes or mold around a skewer in a sausage shape. Preheat oven to broil or prepare barbecue grill with medium-hot coals. Place meat under broiler or on grill 4 inches from source of heat. Cook, turning as necessary, until browned on all sides, about 5 minutes. Cut onion in half lengthwise, then slice to make long, thin strips. Combine cabbage, onion strips, tomato, lemon juice, olive oil and salt to taste in a medium bowl. Toss to mix well. Place 2 or 4 cooked sausage shapes on each pita bread or tortilla. Top with cabbage mixture. Sprinkle with paprika. Serve immediately. Makes 6 sandwiches.

Variation
✳ Greek-Style Hamburgers: Shape meat mixture into hamburger patties. Serve on hamburger buns with desired toppings.

Soft Bread Sheets
Khubz Mar'ook (Lebanon)

A wok supplies the dome shape required for cooking this oversized bread.

Arabic Pocket-Bread dough, below	*All-purpose flour*
	Oil for wok

If using a new wok, season it according to manufacturer's directions. Be sure to scour the outside of your wok well during the seasoning process. Prepare dough up to the point of shaping into balls. Pinch off pieces of dough 3 inches in diameter. Place on a floured surface. Sprinkle with flour. Roll out each piece to a circle 12 inches in diameter. Place backs of your hands under dough and stretch circle to about 20 inches. Let rest 10 minutes on a pillow or cushion covered with a clean cloth. Invert a well-cleaned wok with handles over medium-high heat. Lightly oil outside of wok. Heat until a drop of water sizzles on bottom of inverted wok. Place an enlarged dough circle on hot wok. Cook until dough is browned underneath. Turn and brown lightly on other side. Bread will be soft and floppy. Fold hot bread and place in a plastic bag. Serve warm. Or cool in bag and refrigerate. If baking is preferred, preheat oven to 450F (230C). Place dough circle on a lightly floured board. Slide circle off board onto oven floor. Bake 5 minutes or until set. Place pale-side up under broiler to brown, if desired. Makes 8 to 10 bread sheets.

Arabic Pocket Bread
Khubz Arabi (Arabic)

As the bread cooks, it puffs, forming a pocket for stuffing.

2-1/2 cups warm water (110F, 45C)	*1 tablespoon salt*
	About 6 cups all-purpose flour, sifted
2 (1/4-oz.) pkgs. active dry yeast (2 tablespoons)	*2 tablespoons vegetable oil*

Pour warm water into a large bowl. Sprinkle yeast over water. Stir until dissolved. Add salt. Gradually add 6 cups flour and oil, kneading constantly, until dough is smooth and elastic. If dough sticks to your hands, add more flour. Place in a large greased bowl. Turn dough to grease all sides. Cover with a dry cloth towel and let rise in a warm place until doubled in bulk, about 1-1/2 hours. Punch down gently. Preheat oven to 375F (190C). Divide dough into 24 equal portions. If large pocket breads are preferred, divide into 12 portions. Shape each portion into a smooth ball. Place on a floured surface. Sprinkle tops lightly with flour and cover with a dry cloth towel.

Let rest 15 minutes. Grease baking sheets. Roll out each portion of dough to a 6-inch circle for small pocket breads or a 14-inch circle for large. Place on prepared baking sheets. Bake 10 to 12 minutes for small pocket breads, 12 to 15 minutes for large pocket breads or until bread puffs. If desired, place pale-side up under broiler to brown slightly. Place hot bread immediately in a plastic bag. Serve warm. Or cool in bag and refrigerate. Makes 12 or 24 pocket breads.

Pocket-Bread Sandwiches

Pocket bread lends itself to numerous sandwich combinations. Sample some of these popular pita fillings with their appropriate sauces and relishes.

＊ **Ground-Meat-Kebab Sandwich.** *Chopped lettuce, diced tomato, Ground-Meat Kebabs, pg 89, sliced dill pickle, Hot Sauce, pg 42, or harissa, chopped green onion*

＊ **Egg Sandwich.** *Chopped lettuce, Herb & Nut Omelets (individual), pg 113, diced tomato, sliced dill pickle, Sesame-Seed Sauce, pg 41, chopped green onion*

＊ **Souvlaki Sandwich.** *Shish Kebabs, pg 94, chopped lettuce, diced tomatoes, diced green onion, Garlic Sauce, pg 43*

＊ **Roast-Beef Sandwich.** *Chopped lettuce, roast-beef slices, Zucchini-Relish Salad, pg 36, Garlic Sauce, pg 43, chopped green onion*

Arabic Lamb Pies

Sfeeha (Arabic)

Basic Arabic Pocket-Bread dough is used to make pies of many shapes and with a variety of fillings.

Arabic Pocket-Bread dough, *page 50*	*1/2 cup plain yogurt*
2 lbs. coarsely ground lean lamb	*Salt and freshly ground pepper* *to taste*
1 large onion, grated	*1/2 cup pine nuts*
Juice of 2 lemons (6 tablespoons)	*2 tablespoons olive oil*

Prepare dough up to the point of shaping. Preheat oven to 375F (190C). Lightly grease rimmed baking sheets. Combine lamb, onion, lemon juice, yogurt, salt, pepper and pine nuts in a large bowl. Divide dough into 24 equal portions. Roll out each portion to a 6-inch circle. Place about 1/4 cup meat mixture in center of each circle. Fold 3 sides of circle over filling to make a triangle. Pinch seams together to seal. Arrange meat pies on prepared baking sheets. Bake 20 to 25 minutes or until golden. Remove from oven and brush with olive oil. Pies become darker brown after brushing with olive oil. Immediately remove pies from baking sheets. Makes 24 pies.

Sesame Bread Rings
Cheoreg (Armenia)

Chewy bread rings, or baguettes, are a close cousin to the bagel.

1 cup warm milk (110F, 45C)
1 (1/4-oz.) pkg. active dry yeast
  (1 tablespoon)
1/2 cup butter or margarine
3 eggs, beaten
1 teaspoon salt
1 teaspoon sugar

1 teaspoon ground black-cherry
  kernels (mahlab), if desired
About 5 cups all-purpose flour
1 egg
1 tablespoon water
1/2 cup sesame seeds
1/4 cup water

Pour warm milk into a large bowl. Sprinkle yeast over milk. Stir until dissolved. Add butter or margarine, 3 beaten eggs, salt, sugar and ground cherry kernels, if desired. Mix well. Add about 5 cups flour or enough to make a soft dough that does not stick to your hands. Turn out onto a floured surface. Knead until dough is smooth and elastic. Place in a large greased bowl. Turn dough to grease all sides. Cover with a dry cloth towel. Let rise until doubled in bulk, about 1 hour. Preheat oven to 350F (175C). Lightly grease 2 large baking sheets. Pinch off pieces of dough about 2 inches in diameter. Roll into 10-inch ropes. Shape each rope into a ring slightly overlapping at ends. Pinch ends together. Place on prepared baking sheets. Mix 1 egg with 1 tablespoon water. Brush over rings. Sprinkle each ring with about 1 teaspoon sesame seeds. Bake 15 to 20 minutes or until golden brown, brushing occasionally with some of the 1/4 cup water to crisp top. Remove from baking sheets and cool on racks. Serve warm or wrap cooled bread in plastic wrap and refrigerate. Makes about 25 rings.

Variation
✻ Sesame Baguettes: Instead of shaping ropes into rings, taper ropes at each end. Place on baking sheet. Brush with egg wash and sprinkle with sesame seeds. Bake as directed for rings.

Greek Holiday Bread
Tsourekia (Greece)

Mary Deamos of Pasadena shared her recipe for a festive bread.

1 cup warm water (110F, 45C)	1-1/2 cups sugar
2 (1/4-oz.) pkgs. active dry yeast	2 large eggs
(2 tablespoons)	1/2 cup orange juice
Pinch of sugar	About 9 cups all-purpose flour
2 cups milk	1 egg, beaten
1/4 cup butter or margarine	1/4 cup sesame seeds

Pour warm water into a large bowl. Sprinkle yeast over water. Add pinch of sugar. Stir until yeast is dissolved. Combine milk, butter or margarine and 1-1/2 cups sugar in a medium saucepan. Scald by heating mixture until bubbles appear around edges. Beat eggs in a small bowl. Stir in orange juice. Add about 1/2 cup milk mixture to egg mixture. Stir into milk mixture in saucepan until blended. Cool to warm. Add to yeast mixture. Stir until blended. Stir about 9 cups flour into yeast mixture until dough pulls away from side of bowl. Turn out onto a floured surface. Knead, adding more flour if necessary, until dough is smooth and elastic. Shape into a ball. Place in a greased bowl. Turn to grease all sides. Cover with a dry cloth towel and let rise doubled in bulk, about 1 hour. Preheat oven to 350F (175C). Grease baking sheets. Set aside. For large rolls, divide dough into 16 equal pieces and shape as desired. For small rolls, divide dough into 32 equal pieces and shape as desired. For braids, divide dough into 2 equal portions. Divide each portion into 3 equal pieces. Shape each piece into a 12- to 14-inch rope. Pinch ropes together at one end. Braid and pinch ends together. Place on prepared baking sheets. Brush with beaten egg. Sprinkle with sesame seeds. Let rest 30 minutes. Bake large rolls 20 to 30 minutes. Bake small rolls 15 to 20 minutes. Bake braids 30 to 40 minutes. Bread should be golden. Remove from baking sheets and cool on racks. Serve warm. Or wrap cooled bread in plastic wrap and refrigerate. Makes 16 large rolls, 32 small rolls or 2 braids.

Variation

✳ Greek Easter Braid: Shape rolls and braid as directed. Insert colored hard-cooked eggs in braid indentations. Bake as directed.

VEGETABLES, RICE & GRAINS

Vegetables

Greek and Turkish cooks are masters at vegetable cooking. Vegetables may be cooked to a soft stew in olive oil, stuffed with rice or meat, fried or grilled on an open fire. The seasoning is simple with salt and pepper. Often a vegetable dish relies on the addition of a yogurt topping to round out flavors to perfection.

Stuffing vegetables expands the function of simple vegetables and no one prepares stuffed vegetables more innovatively than a Middle Easterner. Stuffed vegetables may be served hot or cold and made in quantities that will supplement lunch the next day or be served to unexpected guests. For vegetarians, peppers, tomatoes or cabbage stuffed with rice or grains, such as bulgur, makes a delightfully nourishing main dish. Arabs were the first to import eggplant to the Middle East and from there to Spain. The Moors of Andulusia in Spain introduced eggplant to the Mediterranean region. A particularly interesting and satisfying eggplant casserole is Moussaka from Greece.

Because meat is a rare commodity for many Middle Easterners, vegetarian dishes flourish. Plant proteins are classified as incomplete protein because they are deficient in one or more of the essential amino acids. Combining different protein foods, such as legumes with nuts, cereals with beans, and grains with legumes, boosts the protein value of each dish. In Egypt the national bean dish, Fool, has been a mainstay of the diet since the days of the pharoahs. The beans overnight cook in huge narrow-necked vats. By morning they are ready to ladle into plates to eat as Egyptians like best—dressed with oil and lemon juice and some green onion. Be warned that some people lack an enzyme which is necessary for the digestion of fava beans. They may suffer anything from mild discomfort to an extreme toxic reaction from eating this type of bean. If you suspect—through heredity or from your own experience—that you have this problem, avoid eating fava beans.

55

Falafels which are bean patties or balls have replaced meat in the Middle Eastern diet for thousands of years. Today, falafel has reached Western shores and can be found at falafel stands and Middle Eastern restaurants throughout the Western world.

Grains, Rice and Pasta

Wheat and rice dishes dominate in all cuisines of the Mideast-Mediterranean cuisines. Wheat in the form of *bulgur*, from the Arabic word *burghul*, is cooked like rice, using the same proportions of liquid to bulk.

Bulgur is available in many grades. Very fine is classified as number 1. Coarse bulgur is called number 4. The finest grade is mainly eaten raw, as in Parsley Wheat Salad, *Taboulleh*. Bulgur can be eaten plain and topped with a pat of butter, laced with tomato or meat sauce, covered with a thick stew or served as a stuffing for meat, poultry or turkey or vegetables. It can be mixed to make a nutritious, inexpensive meatless hamburger or meatloaf.

Rice, *roz* to Arabs, *pilav* to Turks and *chelo* or *pollo* to Persians, is the queen of grains in Mideast cuisines. A meal in Turkey, Egypt or Iran is incomplete without rice in one or more forms. In the Gulf States, long-grain rice is preferred. Basmati rice from India and Pakistan is a favorite, as is the high-grade long-grain Southern rice from the United States. Thailand and China supply short-grain rice. But converted rice, a product of modern technology, is gaining in popularity in countries such as Iraq where taste for modern processed foods is growing. Converted rice is steamed before milling to enable it to retain much of the natural vitamin and mineral content normally lost in processing. This rice requires a longer cooking time than regular rice and takes 2-1/2 parts liquid to 1 part rice, compared with 2-to-1 ratio for regular rice. To keep rice kernels

MENU

Vegetarian's Delight

Pocket Bread Salad,
page 38

Mixed-Vegetable Casserole
page 58

Cracker Bread,
page 46

Butter Rings,
page 130

Tea

from sticking, Persians and other Middle Eastern cooks wrap a clean cloth towel around the lid and tie the ends around the handle. The toweled lid is placed over the simmering rice 10 minutes before it is done or just after it is done to absorb excess moisture. It really works! See the illustration on page 71.

Couscous, the preferred grain of North Africa, is actually semolina, a byproduct in the manufacture of flour. Made of coarsely crushed heart of durum wheat, it is used mainly in pasta-making and in place of farina in puddings. When making puddings with semolina, use the finest grade which can be purchased in bulk.

Couscous, like bulgur, goes through a steaming and drying process. It, too, comes in several grades from fine to pellet-size. The most popular grade for the dish called *couscous* is found in packaged form at most gourmet grocery stores or Middle Eastern food markets. In North Africa a double-boiler called a *couscousière* holds a perforated basket in which the couscous is steam-cooked over simmering broth. The broth does double duty in cooking vegetables and meat while the couscous steams above.

Although pasta was once regarded as a rarity in Mideast cooking, most countries of the Mediterranean make inspired use of it. Greece, which has culturally faced both East and West, boasts a layered Macaroni Casserole called *Pastitsio*. In Libya, pasta dishes emerged during Italian colonization and are still enjoyed.

Eggplant Purée
Hünkar Beğuendi (Turkey)

This excellent purée, called Sultan's Delight, is usually served as a bed for stews or roast chicken.

1 large eggplant
1/4 cup butter or margarine
1/4 cup all-purpose flour
1 cup milk or half and half

1/2 cup grated Parmesan cheese (1-1/2 oz.)
Salt and freshly ground white pepper to taste

Pierce eggplant in several places. Preheat oven to 400F (205C). Place pierced eggplant on oven rack and bake 1 hour or until soft. If using microwave oven, pierce eggplant and microwave at full power (HIGH) 5 to 7 minutes, depending on size. Peel softened eggplant. Place pulp in a bowl and mash. Set aside. Melt butter or margarine in a medium saucepan over low heat. Stir in flour until smooth. Gradually add milk or half and half. Cook, stirring constantly, until mixture is thickened and smooth, about 5 minutes. Stir in cheese, salt and pepper. Fold in mashed eggplant. Cook, stirring constantly, until thickened, about 3 minutes. Do not scorch. Serve immediately. Makes 6 to 8 servings.

Mixed-Vegetable Casserole
Türlü (Turkey)

Any seasonal vegetables may be used for this casserole.

2 large potatoes, peeled, thickly sliced	2 onions, thinly sliced
2 medium zucchini, thickly sliced	Salt and freshly ground pepper to taste
1 lb. green beans, cleaned, trimmed, or 1 (10-oz.) pkg. frozen cut green beans, thawed	1/2 cup chopped fresh parsley
	1/4 cup chopped fresh dill or 2 tablespoons dill weed
	4 medium tomatoes, diced
1 lb. okra, trimmed, or 1 (10-oz.) pkg. frozen okra, thawed	1 cup Chicken Broth, page 29, or water
	1/3 cup olive oil

Preheat oven to 350F (175C). Arrange layers of potatoes, zucchini, green beans, okra and onions in a large baking pan. Sprinkle with salt and pepper, parsley and dill. Top with tomatoes. Carefully pour broth or water into casserole. Sprinkle with olive oil. Cover. Bake 1-1/4 to 1-1/2 hours or until vegetables are tender. Serve hot. Makes 10 to 12 servings. (See next page for variations.)

Variations

✴ Vegetable Casserole with Eggplant: Substitute 1 small unpeeled eggplant, sliced, for green beans or okra. If desired, sauté eggplant slices in oil before adding to casserole.

✴ Vegetable Casserole with Green Peppers: Substitute 2 large green bell peppers, sliced, for okra or green beans. If desired, sauté pepper slices in oil before adding to casserole.

Eggplant Casserole
Moussaka (Greece)

A delicious and inexpensive Greek classic!

Meat Sauce, see below
Cream Sauce, see below
2 large eggplants, unpeeled
Salt
Oil for frying
1/4 cup grated Parmesan
* cheese (3/4 oz.)*

Meat Sauce:
2 tablespoons butter or
* margarine*
1 onion, chopped
1-1/2 lbs. ground lean beef
1/2 teaspoon ground cinnamon
Pinch of sugar
1/2 cup chopped fresh parsley
Salt and freshly ground pepper
* to taste*
2 tablespoons tomato paste

Cream Sauce:
2-1/2 cups milk
6 tablespoons butter or
* margarine*
1/2 cup all-purpose flour
6 egg yolks
Pinch of ground nutmeg
1/4 cup grated Parmesan
* cheese (3/4 oz.)*
Salt and freshly ground white
* pepper to taste*

Prepare Meat Sauce and Cream Sauce. Set aside. Cut eggplants crosswise into 1/2-inch slices. Sprinkle lightly with salt. Let stand 15 minutes to leach out bitter flavor. Drain and pat dry with paper towels. Pour oil 1/2 inch deep into a large skillet. Heat to 365F (185C) on a deep-fry thermometer. At this temperature, a 1-inch cube of bread will turn golden brown in 60 seconds. Fry 3 or 4 eggplant slices at a time, turning once, until golden on both sides. Add more oil as needed. Drain on paper towels. Preheat oven to 350F (175C). Arrange a third of the fried-eggplant slices in a single layer in a 13" x 9" baking pan. Sprinkle with 2 tablespoons Parmesan cheese. Pour half the Meat Sauce over eggplant layer. Place another third of the eggplant slices over Meat Sauce. Top with remaining Meat Sauce and eggplant slices. Spread Cream Sauce evenly over eggplant slices. Sprinkle with remaining Parmesan cheese. Bake 1 hour or until top is golden brown and bubbly. Serve hot. Makes 8 to 12 servings.

Meat Sauce:
Melt butter or margarine in a large saucepan or skillet. Add onion. Sauté until tender. Add beef, cinnamon, sugar, parsley, salt and pepper. Cook until meat is browned and crumbly. Stir in tomato paste. Cook 5 minutes to blend flavors. Makes about 3 cups.

Cream Sauce:
In a 1-quart saucepan, heat milk until bubbles appear around edges. Melt butter or margarine in a large saucepan. Stir in flour until smooth. Stir over low heat until mixture is golden. Gradually stir in hot milk. Cook, stirring constantly, until thickened. Remove from heat. Beat egg yolks in a small bowl. Stir a small amount of milk mixture into beaten egg yolks. Add egg mixture to hot-milk mixture in saucepan. Stir in nutmeg, Parmesan cheese, salt and pepper. Return to heat. Cook and stir until sauce is smooth and thickened. Makes about 3 cups.

Eggplant slices may be broiled instead of fried. Brush each slice with oil. Place on broiler rack 3 inches from source of heat. Broil until golden. Turn and broil other side until golden.

Fainting Imam
Patlican Imam Bayildi (Turkey)

According to legend, the Imam, or Moslem priest, was so enchanted by this stuffed eggplant, he swooned.

8 Japanese eggplants
3 medium onions
1/2 cup vegetable oil
2 medium tomatoes, diced
2 medium green or red bell peppers, cut in 3" x 1/4" strips
1 small red or yellow hot pepper, seeded, minced
2 tablespoons chopped fresh parsley

5 garlic cloves, minced
Salt and freshly ground black pepper to taste
2 tablespoons olive oil
1-1/2 cups Beef or Chicken Broth, page 29
Juice of 1/2 lemon (1-1/2 tablespoons)
1 teaspoon sugar

Rinse eggplants and pat dry. Slit each eggplant lengthwise from end to end almost all the way through. Cut onions in half lengthwise, then slice to make long, thin strips. Heat vegetable oil in a large skillet. Add eggplants. Cook over medium-high heat, turning frequently to blister on all sides, about 2 minutes. Drain on paper towels. Add onion strips, half the tomatoes, bell peppers, hot pepper, parsley, garlic, salt and black pepper. Sauté until onions are barely tender. Set aside. Preheat oven to 350F (175C). Grease a large baking pan. Place eggplants in prepared baking pan slit-side up. Spoon onion mixture into each slit, pressing with spoon to pack tightly. Sprinkle stuffing with olive oil. Top with remaining tomatoes. Pour broth into pan. Sprinkle eggplants with lemon juice and sugar. Cover. Bake 40 minutes to 1 hour or until eggplants and stuffing are very soft. Makes 8 servings.

Vegetarian Skillet
Shakchoukah (Israel)

From North Africa to Jerusalem, vegetables and eggs are served on toast, over rice or in Arabic pocket bread.

1/2 cup olive oil
1 garlic clove
2 medium onions, thinly sliced
1/2 cup Chicken Broth, page 29, or water
2 medium green bell peppers, diced
2 large potatoes, cubed
4 medium tomatoes, diced

2 medium zucchini, diced
Salt and freshly ground black pepper to taste
1/2 small eggplant, if desired, unpeeled, diced
6 to 8 eggs
Freshly ground black pepper to taste

Heat olive oil in a large skillet. Add garlic. Cook until golden. Discard garlic. Add onions to hot oil. Sauté until tender. Add broth or water, green peppers, potatoes, tomatoes, zucchini, salt and black pepper. Add eggplant, if desired. Mix well. Cover. Cook over medium-low heat, stirring occasionally, until vegetables are almost tender, 30 to 40 minutes. Break eggs over vegetables, spacing them evenly around skillet. Cover. Simmer over low heat until eggs are poached as desired, about 4 minutes. For each serving, use a spatula to serve vegetable mixture with an egg on top. Sprinkle with black pepper to taste. Makes 6 to 8 servings.

Stuffed Peppers
Dolmeh-ye Felfel Sabz (Iran)

Combining dill and mint may seem unusual—but the resulting flavor is superb.

*2 tablespoons butter or
    margarine*
1 large onion, chopped
1/2 lb. ground lean beef or lamb
1 (8-oz.) can tomato sauce
*Salt and freshly ground black
    pepper to taste*
Pinch of sugar
Grated peel of 1 lemon
Juice of 1 lemon (3 tablespoons)
1 cup converted rice
*1-1/2 cups Beef or Chicken
    Broth, page 29*

1 cup chopped fresh parsley
1 cup chopped green onions
*1/2 cup fresh dill leaves or
    2 tablespoons dill weed*
*1 teaspoon crushed dried-leaf
    tarragon*
*1 tablespoon chopped fresh mint
    or 1 teaspoon crushed dried-
    leaf mint*
6 large green or red bell peppers
1 cup Beef Broth, page 29
*2 tablespoons butter or
    margarine*

Melt 2 tablespoons butter or margarine in a large saucepan. Add onion. Sauté until tender. Add meat. Cook until browned and crumbly. Add half the tomato sauce, salt and black pepper. Cook 1 minute. Add sugar, lemon peel, lemon juice and rice. Cook and stir until rice glistens. Add 1-1/2 cups broth. Bring to a boil. Reduce heat and cover. Simmer over low heat 10 minutes or until liquid is almost absorbed. Stir in parsley, green onions, dill, tarragon and mint. Cook 5 minutes. Preheat oven to 350F (175C). Cut a thin slice from stem end of each pepper; reserve to use as lids. Remove seeds and white membrane from peppers. Place peppers in a large baking pan. Spoon meat mixture into peppers. Combine remaining ingredients, including remaining tomato sauce, in a small saucepan. Heat until butter or margarine melts. Pour over stuffed peppers. Cover with reserved lids. Cover baking pan with foil. Bake 1 hour or until peppers are tender and filling is done. Makes 6 servings.

Variations
✳ Stuffed Cabbage: Cook 1 whole medium cabbage in boiling water 8 to 10 minutes, depending on size. Drain and cool. Separate leaves. Place 1 tablespoon filling on each leaf. Roll up, tucking in edges. Place cabbage rolls in a large baking pan, making a single layer. Continue with recipe.
✳ Stuffed Tomatoes: Substitute 8 large tomatoes for the green peppers. Cut a thin slice from each stem end. Scoop out pulp. Add to

meat mixture. Heat 5 minutes before stuffing tomatoes. Continue with recipe.

✳ Stuffed Eggplant: Substitute 8 long Japanese eggplants for the green peppers. Slit each eggplant lengthwise without cutting all the way through. Heat 1/2 cup vegetable oil in a large skillet. Cook each eggplant in hot oil until blistered on all sides. Remove from skillet. Drain on paper towels and let cool. Stuff with meat mixture. Continue with recipe.

Egyptian Beans
Fool Medames (Egypt)

The Egyptian national dish is eaten for breakfast or any time of day with green onions and bread.

1 lb. dried small fava beans or *pink beans, sorted, rinsed*	*1/4 cup olive oil*
Lightly salted water	*1/2 teaspoon ground cumin*
1/2 cup red lentils	*Salt and freshly ground pepper* *to taste*
Juice of 1 lemon (3 tablespoons)	*1/2 cup chopped green onions*

Place beans in a large saucepan. Add lightly salted water to cover. Bring to a boil. Reduce heat and cover. Simmer over low heat 2-1/2 hours. If necessary, add more water to keep beans covered. Add lentils. Cover. Simmer 30 minutes longer or until lentils and beans are tender and mixture is thick but not soupy. Stir in lemon juice, olive oil, cumin, salt and pepper. Serve hot. Sprinkle each serving with green onions. Makes 8 to 10 servings.

Egyptian brown beans, or small fava beans, and red lentils are available in most Middle Eastern markets. Or substitute pink beans for the brown beans and brown lentils for the red lentils.

Bulgur Pilaf
Burghul Mfalfal (Arabic)

This basic method for cooking bulgur is similar to cooking rice.

3 tablespoons butter or
  margarine
2 cups coarse-grade bulgur
4 cups Chicken Broth, page 29

Salt and freshly ground pepper
  to taste
2 teaspoons grated lemon peel

Melt butter or margarine in a large saucepan. Add bulgur. Sauté 5 minutes. Add broth, salt and pepper. Bring to a boil. Reduce heat and cover. Simmer over low heat, stirring occasionally, 20 minutes or until bulgur is soft and liquid is absorbed. Stir in lemon peel. Makes 6 servings.

Variations
* Bulgur with Tomato Sauce: Sauté 1 chopped onion in 2 tablespoons butter or margarine until onion is tender. Stir in bulgur. Sauté 2 minutes. Stir in 2 tablespoons tomato paste, 1/2 cup tomato sauce and broth. Cook as directed above.
* Bulgur with Currants & Pine Nuts: Sauté 1 chopped onion, 1/4 cup currants and 2 tablespoons pine nuts in 2 tablespoons butter or margarine until onion is golden. Stir in bulgur. Sauté 2 minutes. Stir in broth. Cook as directed above.

☼ Tunisian Couscous
Couscous Complet Tunisien (Tunisia)

An exquisite party meal made in a special utensil called a *couscousière*.

Stuffed Meatballs, page 87
Carrot & Orange Salad,
    page 36
Zucchini-Relish Salad,
    page 36
Mixed Salad, page 37
2 cups packaged couscous
3 tablespoons vegetable oil
2 cups water
1 tablespoon salt
Water
2 lbs. boneless chuck beef, cubed
1 medium onion, quartered
1/4 cup vegetable oil

1 medium tomato, cut in wedges
1 medium turnip, peeled, cut in
    pieces
4 medium carrots, peeled
2 medium potatoes, peeled, cut
    in wedges
Salt to taste
1 small cabbage, cut in wedges
2 medium zucchini, cut in
    1-inch diagonal slices
6 green onions, sliced
Few sprigs cilantro
Few sprigs parsley
Harissa

Prepare Stuffed Meatballs. Set aside. Prepare Carrot & Orange Salad, Zucchini-Relish Salad and Mixed Salad. Refrigerate. Place couscous in a large bowl. Sprinkle with 3 tablespoons oil. Gradually stir in 2 cups water and 1 tablespoon salt. Rub mixture between palms of your hands to separate grains. Let stand 30 minutes or longer. Fill bottom section of couscousière with water. Add beef, onion, 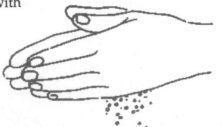 1/4 cup oil, tomato, turnip, carrots, potatoes and salt to taste. If needed, add more water to cover. Bring to a boil. Reduce heat and cover. Cook over medium heat 45 minutes. Add cabbage, zucchini, green onions, cilantro and parsley. Cover and cook over medium-low heat 10 minutes. Place couscous mixture in top section of couscousière. Make a well in center of mixture so steam will circulate while cooking. Fit top section of couscousière over bottom section where soup is cooking. Be sure liquid in bottom section does not touch couscous through perforated base of top section; couscous should cook by steaming. Cover and simmer over low heat 30 minutes.

Turn steamed couscous into a large, shallow platter. Cool slightly. Toss to break up any lumps. If necessary, use your fingers to separate grains. Arrange couscous in a mound on platter. Pour some soup liquid over couscous, if desired. Top with Stuffed Meatballs and meat and vegetables from soup. Pour soup liquid into individual bowls. Place Carrot & Orange Salad, Zucchini-Relish Salad and Mixed Salad in small bowls around platter. To eat, spoon couscous on your plate. Top with meats and vegetables. Ladle soup liquid over couscous on your plate. Season sparingly with harissa. Eat with small servings of each salad. Makes 6 to 8 servings.

Packaged couscous is a granulated pasta (semolina) made from the heart of durum wheat. Harissa is a paste made from hot peppers. Both are available at Middle Eastern grocery stores. Harissa is also available at some gourmet shops. Bottled hot-pepper sauce may be substituted.

Variation
✳ Tunisian Couscous with Barbecued Meats: Grilled or barbecued sausages and baby lamb rib chops may be added to couscous platter.

Egyptian Rice
Roz (Egypt)

This is the rice used at almost every Egyptian meal.

1/4 cup butter or margarine	*2 cups water*
1 cup long-grain rice	*Salt to taste*

Melt butter or margarine in a medium saucepan. Add half the rice. Sauté until rice is transparent. Add remaining rice, water and salt. Bring to a boil. Reduce heat and cover. Simmer over medium heat about 20 minutes or until liquid is absorbed. Makes 4 servings.

Herb Rice
Sabzi Pollo (Iran)

A prized dish among the hundreds of Persian rice recipes.

About 4 cups lightly salted water	*1 bunch parsley, chopped (1 cup)*
2 cups long-grain rice	*2 bunches cilantro, chopped (2 cups)*
1 bunch green onions, green part only, chopped (about 1 cup)	*1/4 cup butter or margarine*

Bring about 4 cups lightly salted water to a boil in a large saucepan. Add rice. Water should cover rice by about 1 inch. Cook, uncovered, over medium heat 10 minutes. Drain. Rinse rice with cold water. Drain again. Combine chopped green onions, parsley and cilantro in a medium bowl. Mix well. Melt butter or margarine in a large saucepan. Add a fourth of the rice. Sprinkle with a third of the herbs. Alternate layers of rice and herbs, ending with rice. Remove from heat. Place a clean cloth towel over saucepan. Place lid on towel. Bring corners of towel up and over top of lid. Fasten securely with a rubber band. Simmer over very low heat 25 to 30 minutes or until rice is soft and fluffy. Makes 6 servings.

☼ Basic Dry Pilaf

Draining cooked rice in a colander produces a slightly dry rice preferred by Mideast and Mediterranean cooks.

8 cups water (2 qts.)
2 teaspoons salt
2 cups converted rice

1/2 cup butter or margarine
Freshly ground pepper to taste

In a medium saucepan, bring water to a boil. Add salt and rice. Reduce heat and cover. Simmer over medium-low heat 20 to 30 minutes or until rice is just tender but not too soft. Drain well in a colander. In the same saucepan, melt butter or margarine over medium heat until golden. Add rice. Toss to coat well. Turn out onto a platter. Sprinkle generously with pepper. Makes 6 to 8 servings.

Variations

✳ Pilaf with Yogurt: Top each serving with 1 or 2 tablespoons yogurt.

✳ Pilaf with Almonds & Raisins: Prepare pilaf, omitting butter or margarine and pepper. In a small skillet, melt 1/2 cup butter or margarine. Add 2 tablespoons sliced almonds, 2 tablespoons seedless raisins and 1 tablespoon shredded orange peel. Sauté until raisins are plumped, about 3 minutes. For a sweet pilaf, add 1/2 teaspoon cinnamon and 1 tablespoon sugar. Fold into pilaf.

☼ Basic Soft Pilaf

Middle Eastern cooks usually stir in another ingredient for increased flavor and texture.

1/4 cup butter or margarine
1 cup converted rice
1 teaspoon salt

2 cups water or Chicken Broth,
*   page 29*

In a medium saucepan, melt butter or margarine over medium

heat. Add rice. Stir and cook 1 minute. Add salt and water or broth. Bring to a boil and cover. Simmer over medium-low heat 20 to 30 minutes or until liquid is absorbed. Makes 4 servings.

Variations

✳ Pilaf with Almonds: Fold 1/4 cup toasted slivered or sliced blanched almonds into hot cooked rice.

✳ Pilaf with Raisins: Fold 1/4 to 1/2 cup seedless raisins into hot cooked rice. Cover and let stand about 10 minutes to plump raisins.

✳ Pilaf with Orange Peel: Stir 2 tablespoons grated orange peel into hot cooked rice.

Lentils & Rice
Mujadarah (Arabic)

This vegetarian dish needs only a salad and Arabic pocket bread to be a complete meal.

1/4 cup butter or margarine
1 medium onion, sliced
1 cup lentils, sorted, rinsed
4 cups Chicken Broth,
*   page 29, or water*
1 cup long-grain rice
1 teaspoon ground cumin
Salt and freshly ground pepper
*   to taste*
6 lemon wedges

Melt butter or margarine in a large saucepan. Add onion. Sauté until onion is tender but not browned. Add lentils. Sauté 1 minute. Add broth or water. Bring to a boil. Reduce heat and cover. Simmer over low heat 20 minutes. Add rice, cumin, salt and pepper. Simmer 30 to 40 minutes or until rice and lentils are tender and liquid is absorbed. Mixture will be mushy. Serve with lemon wedges. Makes 4 to 6 servings.

Variation

✳ Lentils & Rice with Meat or Chicken: Add 2 cups diced, cubed or shredded cooked beef, lamb, veal or chicken to lentil and rice mixture 10 minutes before end of cooking time.

፣፣፣፣፣፣፣፣፣፣፣፣፣፣፣፣፣፣፣፣፣፣፣፣፣፣፣፣፣፣፣፣፣፣፣፣፣፣

Persian Steamed Rice
Chelo (Iran)

An unusual steaming method makes this rice light and fluffy.

About 4 cups lightly salted water
2 cups long-grain rice
2 tablespoons butter or margarine

Salt and freshly ground pepper
to taste

Bring about 4 cups lightly salted water to a boil in a large saucepan. Add rice. Water should cover rice by 2 inches or more. Add more boiling water, if necessary. Cook, uncovered, over medium heat 10 minutes. Drain. Rinse rice with cold water. Drain again. Melt butter or margarine in a large saucepan. Add drained rice. Stir lightly to coat well. Place saucepan lid on a clean cloth towel. Bring corners of towel up and over top of lid. Fasten securely with a rubber band. Place lid firmly on saucepan. Cook over medium-low heat 25 to 30 minutes or until rice is fluffy and water is absorbed. Keep covered until ready to serve. Makes 6 servings.

Variations

✳ Steamed Crusty Rice: Attach towel and lid as directed above. Steam rice a total of 40 to 45 minutes over very low heat or until rice in bottom of saucepan is golden and crusty. Serve rice with pieces of crust lifted from bottom of saucepan.

✳ Steamed Rice with Fruits & Nuts: Sauté 1/4 cup chopped mixed dried fruit, 1/4 cup slivered almonds and 1/4 cup raisins in 1/4 cup butter or margarine. Add drained rice. Sauté 1 minute. Continue with recipe.

✳ Savory Steamed Rice: Sauté 1 chopped onion, 2 tablespoons chopped fresh parsley, 2 tablespoons chopped cilantro, 1/4 tablespoon

Sour-cherry jam is imported from Greece and the former Yugoslavia and is available at Middle Eastern grocery stores. Cherry jam may be substituted.

chopped fresh dill or 1 teaspoon dill weed in 1/4 cup butter or margarine. Add drained rice. Sauté 1 minute. Continue with recipe.

✳ Rice with Sour Cherries (*Alo-baloo Pollo*): Fold about 6 tablespoons sour-cherry jam into 4 cups steamed rice.

☀ Steamed Rice Mold
Pilav (Turkey)

Some of the numerous variations for this molded rice are given below.

2 tablespoons butter or
  margarine
2 cups long-grain rice
3-1/2 cups strong Chicken
  Broth, page 29

Salt and freshly ground pepper
  to taste
Parsley sprigs for garnish

Melt butter or margarine in a large saucepan. Add rice. Sauté 2 minutes or until rice is glazed. Add broth, salt and pepper. Bring to a boil. Reduce heat and cover. Cook over medium heat 25 minutes or until rice is tender and liquid is absorbed. Oil an 8-inch ring mold. Turn cooked rice into mold. Smooth top with the back of a spoon. Cover with a double thickness of waxed paper. Place lid on top. Let stand 10 to 20 minutes to set. Run a metal spatula around inside of mold. Place a platter upside-down over mold. Invert mold and platter. Remove mold. Garnish with parsley sprigs. Makes 6 to 8 servings.

Variations
✳ Rice & Carrot Mold: Sauté 4 grated carrots in 1/4 cup butter or margarine. Sprinkle with 1 teaspoon sugar. Add rice. Sauté 2 minutes to glaze. Continue with recipe.

✳ Rice & Spinach Mold: Omit butter or margarine. Sauté 2 bunches chopped spinach or 1 (10-ounce) package frozen spinach, thawed and squeezed dry, in 1/4 cup olive oil. Add rice. Sauté 2 minutes to glaze. Continue with recipe.

✳ Jeweled Rice Mold: Alternate layers of cooked rice, 1/4 cup chopped mixed dried fruit, 1/4 cup slivered almonds, 1/4 cup raisins or currants in mold. Continue with recipe.

Macaroni Casserole
Pastitsio (Greece)

Thick, Greek-style spaghetti or ziti may be used in this freezer-to-oven party casserole.

Meat Sauce, see below
Cream Sauce, see below
1 lb. large elbow macaroni or
* spaghetti*
1/4 cup butter or margarine,
* melted*
1/2 cup grated Parmesan
* cheese*
1/4 teaspoon ground nutmeg or
* cinnamon*
Pinch of sugar
Salt and freshly ground pepper
* to taste*
3 eggs, beaten
1/4 cup grated Parmesan
* cheese*

Meat Sauce:
2 tablespoons butter or
* margarine*
1 medium onion, chopped
1 garlic clove, minced

1-1/2 lbs. ground lean beef
2 tablespoons tomato paste
1 cup Beef Broth, page 29
2 tablespoons chopped fresh
* parsley*
1/2 teaspoon ground cinnamon,
* if desired*
Pinch of sugar
Salt and freshly ground pepper
* to taste*

Cream Sauce:
3 cups milk
6 tablespoons butter or
* margarine*
1/4 cup all-purpose flour
Pinch of nutmeg
Salt and freshly ground white
* pepper to taste*
6 egg yolks, beaten

Prepare Meat Sauce and Cream Sauce. Cook macaroni or spaghetti as directed on package. Drain. Return drained pasta to pan. Add butter or margarine, 1/2 cup Parmesan cheese, nutmeg or cinnamon, sugar, salt and pepper. Toss gently. Add eggs. Toss to coat pasta well. Set aside. Preheat oven to 350F (175C). Grease a 13" x 9" baking pan. Spread half the pasta mixture evenly in baking pan. Spoon Meat Sauce over pasta. Top with remaining pasta mixture. Pour Cream Sauce evenly over pasta layer. Sprinkle with 1/4 cup Parmesan cheese. Bake 50 to 55 minutes or until golden. Cut into 3-inch squares and serve immediately. Makes 12 servings.

Meat Sauce:
Melt butter or margarine in a large skillet. Add onion and garlic. Sauté until onion is tender. Add beef. Cook until browned and crumbly. Stir in tomato paste. Add remaining ingredients. Cover and simmer over low heat 20 minutes. Makes about 3 cups.

Cream Sauce:
Scald milk by heating in a medium saucepan over medium heat until bubbles appear around edge. Melt butter or margarine in another medium saucepan over low heat. Stir in flour. Cook and stir 2 minutes. Gradually add scalded milk. Stir over low heat until mixture comes to a boil. Boil 1 minute, stirring constantly. Stir in nutmeg, salt and pepper. Cool slightly. Gradually stir in egg yolks until sauce is smooth. Makes about 4 cups.

Variation
✳ Greek-Style Lasagna: Substitute 1 pound lasagna noodles for elbow macaroni or spaghetti. Cook as directed on package. Continue with recipe, layering noodles lengthwise in casserole.

Stuffed Potatoes
Kubbat at Batata (Kuwait)

These torpedo-shaped croquettes are served as an appetizer or main dish throughout the Arab world.

1/2 pound chopped lamb or beef	*4 potatoes, peeled and*
1 onion, chopped	*quartered*
1/4 cup chopped parsley	*1/2 teaspoon turmeric*
2 cloves garlic, minced	*Oil or shortening for deep-*
Salt to taste	*frying*
1/2 cup rice	

Combine meat and onion in skillet. Cook and stir until meat is crumbly and browned. Add parsley, garlic and season with salt. Cook rice with potatoes in water to cover until potatoes are just tender. Drain. Cool slightly. Place potatoes and rice in a bowl. Add turmeric and season with salt to taste. Mash until smooth. Cool. Pinch off portion of potato mixture about the size of an egg. Form into deep cup, using thumb to shape cup. Stuff cavity with meat mixture. Pinch together opening to seal, then roll in palms of hand to form into oval-shaped ball with tapered ends. Heat oil until medium-hot. Add stuffed potatoes and fry until golden on all sides. Drain on paper towel. Makes 6 servings.

Variation
This variation will remind you of English Shepherd's Pie.
✳ Iraqi Potato-Beef Casserole *(Kibbe Batata)*: Spread half the potato mixture in a greased 13" x 9" baking pan. Spread the meat filling over potato layer. Top with remaining potato mixture and sprinkle with cinnamon, if desired. Dot with 2 tablespoons butter or margarine. Bake at 350F (175C) 30 to 40 minutes or until golden. Cut into squares or diamonds to serve.

ꭱꭱꭱꭱꭱꭱꭱꭱꭱꭱꭱꭱꭱꭱꭱꭱꭱꭱꭱꭱꭱꭱꭱꭱꭱꭱꭱꭱꭱ

☼ Vegetarian Lentils, Pasta & Rice
Koushari (Egypt)

A salad and crusty bread will complete this vegetarian meal-in-a-dish.

1/4 cup olive oil
1 large onion, chopped
2 garlic cloves, minced
1 cup lentils, rinsed
1 (8-oz.) can tomato sauce
4 cups Chicken Broth, page 29
   or water
2 cups cooked elbow or tube
   macaroni

2 cups cooked long-grain rice
Salt and freshly ground pepper
   to taste
1 tablespoon chopped fresh
   parsley
Lemon wedges for garnish

Heat olive oil in a large suacepan. Add onion and garlic. Sauté onion is tender. Add lentils. Sauté 1 minute. Stir in tomato sauce. Cook 1 minute to blend flavors. Add broth or water. Bring to a boil. Reduce heat and cover. Cook over medium-low heat 40 minutes or until lentils are tender. Fold in cooked macaroni, rice, salt and pepper. Heat through, stirring frequently. Garnish with parsley and lemon wedges. Makes 6 to 8 servings.

Variation
✳ Baked lentil, Pasta & Rice Casserole: In a small skillet, sauté onion and garlic in olive oil. Add lentils. Sauté 1 minute. Add tomato sauce. Place lentil mixture in a large baking pan. Add 4 cups broth or water. Cover. Bake at 350F (175C) until lentils are tender, about 1 hour. Add cooked macaroni, rice, salt and pepper. Cover and bake 15 minutes longer or until heated through. Garnish as desired.

FILO DISHES

The dough that is so fine you can see your hand through it is called *filo* from *phyllo,* the Greek word for leaf.

Origins of filo are unknown. Filo has travelled far and wide over the centuries. Marching Byzantine, Islamic and Ottoman armies spread filo to Europe and North Africa. In France, the invention of puff pastry was an attempt to copy flaky filo pastry used by Moors. However, it is probably impossible to trace the evolutionary process of several thousand years to a single source. Some authorities theorize that the Byzantines, who were innovative bakers, refined the thin dough they used to enclose foods. Others speculate that Middle Eastern and Oriental spice traders sparked the adaptation of the thin dough similar to Chinese wonton wrappers and egg-roll skins.

Filo pastry is known by many names: *ouaraka* in Morocco, *yufka* or *baklava hamaru* in Turkey, *peta* in the Balkan Peninsula and *strudel* in Central Europe. Pastries are called *breik* in Tunisia, *bourek* in Algeria, *borekia* in turkey, *bourekia* in Greece and *sambousik* or *mutabbaq* in Arabic countries.

The method for preparing filo pastry has not changed since ancient times in the households where the art is still practiced. The basic flour-water dough is rolled out into a large circle with a dowel to no more than 1/8-inch thickness. Instead of rolling out the dough, some cooks choose to stretch it by hand on a long table. Happily, filo sheets can be purchased at any Mideast or Mediterranean food market. Today filo can be found in dairy cases of many supermarkets. Most packages contain 18 to 20 sheets, varying in thickness, depending on the individual manufacturer.

Although working with filo is easy, there are some ground rules to observe. Avoid using dough that has become dry or crumbles and flakes easily. Filo can be stored up to one month in the refrigerator, or longer in the freezer. It can be used as needed, provided the sheets are wrapped airtight and are fresh to begin with. If your newly purchased filo is too dry or moldy, return or discard it.

Despite its fragile texture, filo is a hardy material with a high tolerance for abuse. Tears may be patched with a small piece of moistened filo. Crinkles can be patted or smoothed down. Somewhat dry sheets can be revived by misting them lightly with water from a spray bottle. Filo can be molded against almost any shape. Any filling can be used with filo. Try your own inventive concoctions.

When using filo, either butter or oil is recommended for brushing to keep the dough from drying and flaking. Oil is usually preferred for savory pastries using vegetables or grains. But butter or margarine can be used as well. Clarifying the butter not only removes the milky, rather gritty residue, but enhances flavor. If clarifying butter poses a problem, use melted butter or margarine.

MENU

Holiday Delight

Pistachio Nuts, Olives

Wrapped Cheese Pie
page 79

Spinach Pie
page 80

Fried Meatballs,
page 91

Shrimp & Feta Bake,
page 110

Deluxe Baklava, page 129

Fried Curls, page 127

☀ Wrapped Cheese Pie
Tyropita (Greece)

My sister Mary Thomas uses this method of wrapping the pastry around the filling.

6 eggs
1 cup milk or plain yogurt
2 lbs. feta cheese, crumbled
1/4 cup chopped fresh dill or
* 1 tablespoon dill weed*

Freshly ground white pepper to
* taste*
1 lb. filo pastry sheets
1/2 cup butter, clarified,
* page 129, or margarine,*
* melted*

Beat eggs in a large bowl. Blend in milk or yogurt. Stir in feta cheese, dill and pepper. Mix well. Preheat oven to 350F (175C). Butter a 13" x 9" baking pan. Brush 1 filo pastry sheet with clarified butter or melted margarine. Place in baking pan, allowing overhang all around. Set aside 2 filo sheets and cover with plastic wrap to prevent drying out. Place remaining filo sheets over first sheet, brushing each with butter or margarine. Spread cheese filling over filo layers. Bring overhanging ends of filo over filling. Smooth creases. Brush with butter or margarine. Top with remaining 2 filo sheets. Trim edges. Brush with butter or margarine. Bake 40 to 50 minutes or until golden brown. Let stand 20 minutes to set before cutting. Cut into 3-inch diamond or square shapes. Makes 12 pieces.

Variation

✻ Cheese Triangles *(Tyrotrigona)*: Cut stacked filo sheets lengthwise in halves, making strips. Use 1 strip for each triangle. Brush strip with clarified butter or melted margarine. Fold lengthwise in half or in thirds to make a long, 2-inch-wide strip. Place 1 teaspoon filling in corner of strip. Fold flag-fashion, by folding corner over filling, making a triangle. Continue folding strip as in a flag-fold, maintaining triangle shape. Brush with butter or margarine. Place on lightly greased baking sheets. Bake at 350F (175C) 10 to 15 minutes or until golden brown. Makes 40 pastries.

Spinach Pie
Spanakopita (Greece)

Most greens and any cheese may be used as a filling for this
famous pie.

2 lbs. fresh spinach or
  2 (10-oz.) pkgs. frozen
  chopped spinach, thawed
6 eggs
1 cup milk
1/2 lb. feta cheese, crumbled
1/4 cup olive oil
2 medium onions, chopped

1/4 cup chopped fresh dill or
  1 tablespoon dill weed
Salt and freshly ground pepper
  to taste
1 lb. filo pastry sheets
1/2 cup olive oil
2 tablespoons cold water

Rinse fresh spinach thoroughly several times. Trim stems and
discard. Chop leaves and drain well. If using frozen spinach, squeeze
dry after thawing and fluff to separate. Beat eggs in a large bowl.
Blend in milk. Stir in feta cheese. Heat 1/4 cup olive oil in a large
skillet. Add spinach and onions. Sauté until spinach wilts, about
2 minutes. Add dill, salt and pepper. Sauté 1 minute to blend flavors.
Add to cheese mixture. Mix well. Set aside. Preheat oven to 350F
(175C). Oil a 13" x 9" baking pan. Stack filo pastry sheets. Trim to fit
pan. Cut in half if sheets are large. Cover with plastic wrap to prevent
drying out. Heat 1 cup olive oil in a small skillet. Place half the filo
sheets in prepared pan, brushing each with hot oil. Pour spinach
mixture over filo layers. Top with remaining filo sheets, brushing
each with hot oil. Brush top sheet with hot oil. Sprinkle with cold
water. Bake 40 to 50 minutes or until golden brown. Let stand 20
minutes to set before cutting. Cut into 3-inch diamond or square
shapes. Makes 12 pieces.

Variations

✳ Spinach Triangles: Use 1 filo pastry sheet for each triangle. Brush
with hot oil. Fold in thirds to make a rectangle 4 inches wide. Brush
again with hot oil. Place 1 mounded tablespoon spinach mixture in
corner of rectangle. Fold flag-fashion, by folding corner over filling,
making a triangle. Continue folding strip as in a flag-fold, maintaining

triangle shape. Brush top with oil. Place on baking sheet. Bake at 350F (175C) 15 to 20 minutes or until golden brown. Makes about 20 triangles.

✳ Spinach Wontons: May be baked or fried. Substitute 1 (12-ounce) package wonton wrappers for filo pastry sheets. Place about 2 teaspoons spinach mixture in center of each wrapper. Fold sides over filling, making rectangles. Moisten edges to seal seams. Place on greased baking sheets. Brush with hot oil. Bake at 350F (175C) 20 to 25 minutes or until golden. To fry: do not brush with oil; heat oil for frying at 275F (135C) on a deep-fry thermometer. Fry wontons until golden on all sides. Drain on paper towels. Makes 50 wontons.

☀ Chicken Pastry
Bastela (Morocco)

For your next party, serve this at a low table. Let everyone sit on high pillows.

1 (2-1/2-lb.) chicken, cut up	8 eggs, beaten
Salt and freshly ground black pepper to taste	2 cups ground toasted almonds, page 46
2 tablespoons peanut oil	1/4 cup granulated sugar
1 medium onion, chopped	1/2 teaspoon ground cinnamon
2 cups Chicken Broth, page 29, or water	7 filo pastry sheets
Pinch of saffron threads or powder, if desired	1/4 cup butter, clarified, page 129, or margarine, melted
1 cinnamon stick	1/4 cup powdered sugar
1/2 cup chopped fresh parsley	Ground cinnamon for garnish
1/2 chopped cilantro	Kumquats for garnish, if desired

Place chicken in a large skillet. Sprinkle with salt and pepper. Pour peanut oil over chicken. Add onion and broth or water. Stir in saffron, if desired. Bring to a boil. Add cinnamon stick. Reduce heat and cover. Simmer over low heat 1 hour or until chicken is very tender. Remove chicken from skillet. Reserve liquid. Cool chicken. Remove meat from bones. Shred chicken into a bowl. Set aside. Remove cinnamon stick from skillet and discard. Measure 1 cup liquid and return to skillet. Bring to a boil. Add parsley and cilantro. Simmer, uncovered, over low heat 3 minutes. Add beaten eggs. Cook and stir until scrambled and liquid is absorbed. Set aside. Combine almonds, granulated sugar and 1/2 teaspoon cinnamon in a small bowl. Set aside. Preheat oven to 350F (175C). Butter a 10-inch ovenproof skillet with rounded sides. Stack filo pastry sheets. Cover with plastic wrap to prevent drying out. Place 4 filo sheets in bottom of skillet, brushing each with clarified butter or melted margarine.

Allow a 5- to 6-inch overhang. Sprinkle a third of the almond mixture over filo sheets. Top with half the shredded chicken. Top with another third of the almond mixture. Drain egg mixture, if necessary. Place half the egg mixture over almond mixture. Repeat until all ingredients are used, ending with almond mixture. Fold overhang over filling. Smooth down creases. Brush with butter or margarine.

Top with remaining 3 filo sheets, brushing each with butter or margarine and folding overhang under. Bake 25 to 35 minutes or until golden brown. Cool slightly. Invert onto a platter. Sprinkle with powdered sugar. Make a decorative crisscross design with remaining cinnamon. Garnish with kumquats, if desired. Cut in wedges and serve hot. Makes about 6 servings.

༆༆༆༆༆༆༆༆༆༆༆༆༆༆༆༆༆༆༆༆༆༆༆༆༆

☼ Filo Triangles
Sambousik (Arabic)

Prepare one of the fillings suggested for these Arabic-style triangles.

Cheese Filling, see below
Meat Filling, see below
Spinach Filling, see below
20 filo pastry sheets
1/3 cup butter, clarified,
  page 129, or margarine,
  melted

1/2 lb. ground lean beef or lamb
2 tablespoons pine nuts
1/4 teaspoon ground allspice
Pinch of cinnamon
Salt and freshly ground pepper
  to taste
2 teaspoons lemon juice

Cheese Filling:
1 cup crumbled feta cheese,
  ricotta cheese, Syrian cheese
  or soft Mexican cheese (about
  4 oz.)
1/2 cup chopped fresh parsley
1 small onion, grated
Salt and freshly ground white
  pepper to taste

Meat Filling:
1 tablespoon butter or
  margarine
1 small onion, chopped

Spinach Filling:
1 lb. fresh spinach or
  1 (10-oz.) pkg. frozen
  chopped spinach, thawed
1/4 cup olive oil
1 small onion, chopped
1/4 cup crumbled feta cheese,
  cottage cheese or soft
  Mexican cheese (1 oz.)
Juice of 1 lemon (3 tablespoons)
1/4 teaspoon sumac
Salt and freshly ground black
  pepper to taste

Prepare desired filling. Set aside. Preheat oven to 350F (175C). Stack filo pastry sheets and cut lengthwise into thirds, making long, thin strips. Stack strips. Cover with plastic wrap to prevent drying. Use 3 strips of filo for each triangle. Stack 3 strips, brushing each with clarified butter or melted margarine. Place 1 heaping tablespoon filling in corner of strip. Fold flag-fashion, opposite, to make a triangle. Place seam-side down on baking sheets. Brush tops with butter or margarine. Bake 15 to 20 minutes or until golden. Makes 20 triangles.

Cheese Filling:

Combine all ingredients in a medium bowl. Mix well.

Meat Filling:

Melt butter or margarine in a small saucepan. Add onion. Sauté until tender. Add meat. Cook until just browned. Add remaining ingredients. Cook and stir 2 minutes.

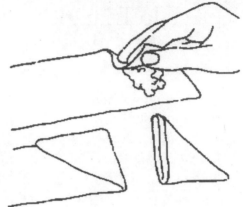

Spinach Filling:

Rinse fresh spinach thoroughly several times. Trim off stems and discard. Chop leaves and drain well. If using frozen spinach, squeeze dry after thawing and fluff to separate. Place spinach in a large bowl. Heat olive oil in a small skillet. Add onion. Sauté 1 minute. Add to spinach. Add remaining ingredients. Toss gently to mix well.

MEATS

Lamb is king of meats in Mideast cooking. It is a symbol of religious sacrifice, celebration and hospitality, as well a staple of the diet.

Arabs have created a luxurious meal of whole, stuffed lamb, called *oozi*. The entire meal is presented on large pieces of flat bread laid on a huge tray, with satellite dishes of tomatoes, cucumbers, cooked squash and seasonal fruit. The idea can be achieved by roasting leg or shoulder of lamb and serving it over large sheets of soft flat bread laid on a large serving tray and surrounded with seasoned fruit and salads or cooked vegetables. Roast Lamb with Potatoes and Roast Leg of Lamb with Orzo offer additional ways to serve roast lamb.

Kebabs, whether made with ground lamb or chunks, were created by meat-eating tribes who cut meat into bite-size pieces so it would be easier to eat with fingers or enclose in pieces of bread. Today incredible varieties of kebabs have made their way around the world to the delight of modern cooks looking for an easy yet glamorous way to serve appetizers or most any grilled meat, fish or poultry.

Cooks from the Arabic world have developed unlimited ground-meat specialties. Meat called *kibbe* may be shaped into balls, patties, sausages or torpedoes. They may be stuffed, baked, boiled, broiled or fried. For centuries Arab women spent hours over mortars and pestles grinding meat—until the food processor came along. The versatile meat cakes freeze well and can be prepared in almost any size and shape in large quantities.

Stews abound throughout the Mideast-Mediterranean cuisines and some of the most innovative are the North African tajine, which are meats cooked and served in cone-shaped pottery also called a *tajine*. Greeks and Turks are flavor magicians when it

MENU
Arabian Nights Feast

Garbanzo-Bean Dip, page 22

Yogurt Cheese, page 131

Parsley-Wheat Salad, page 37

Arabic Pocket Bread, page 50

Roast Leg of Lamb

Bulgur Pilaf, page 65

Dried Fruit

Shredded-Pastry Dessert,
page 120

Tea

Arabic Coffee

comes to seasoning stews. Greek *Yahni* is a basic recipe to which almost any vegetable may be added.

Organ meats, such as liver, tripe, heart, lung, kidney, brains and sweetbreads are widely used. Every scrap of lamb—or in desert lands, camel—is utilized. It is considered sacrilegious to waste any portion of an animal which provides cloth, labor and food to man.

Stuffed Meatballs
Kubbe (Iraq)

These stuffed meat patties are always part of an Iraqi buffet.

Kubbe Filling, page 94
1-1/2 lbs. ground extra-lean beef
1 cup medium-grade bulgur
1/2 cup fine-grade semolina or farina

1-1/2 teaspoons baking soda
1 cup water
Salt to taste
Oil for frying

Prepare Kubbe Filling. Set aside. Place ground beef, bulgur, semolina or farina, baking soda, water and salt in food processor. Process until smooth. Pinch off pieces of mixture 2 inches in diameter. Shape into balls. Moisten your hands and mold each ball into a cup shape 1-1/2 inches deep. Place 1 tablespoon Kubbe Filling in each cup. Shape meat mixture around filling, pinching seams together to enclose filling completely. Shape into rounded patties about 2-1/2 inches in diameter. Pour oil about 1 inch deep into a large skillet. Heat to 350F (175C) on a deep-fry thermometer. At this temperature, a 1-inch cube of bread will turn golden brown in 65 seconds. Fry a few meat patties at a time until golden brown on both sides, about 10 minutes. Drain on paper towels. Serve hot. Makes about 20 patties.

Tunisian Meatballs
Boulettes de Viande (Tunisia)

Meatballs are part of Tunisian Couscous, page 66, but may be served by themselves.

1 lb. ground lean veal, lamb or beef	1 (6-inch) celery-heart stalk, cut in 1-inch pieces
3 green onions, chopped	1 small potato, peeled, cut in 6 cubes
1/4 cup chopped fresh parsley	
1 slice French bread or white bread	1 egg
Water	All-purpose flour
2 garlic cloves, minced	Oil for frying
1 egg, beaten	1 (8-oz.) can tomato sauce
Pinch of ground cinnamon	1/4 cup dry red wine
Salt and freshly ground pepper to taste	Salt and freshly ground pepper to taste

Combine meat, green onions and parsley in a large bowl. Moisten bread in water. Squeeze dry. Add to meat mixture. Add garlic, 1 beaten egg, cinnamon, salt and pepper. Mix well. Divide into 6 equal portions. Shape into balls. Insert pieces of celery and potato into center of meatballs. Celery and potato should be completely covered with meat. Beat 1 egg in a shallow bowl. Dip meatballs in beaten egg. Roll in flour. Pour oil 1/2 inch deep into a large skillet. Heat to 350F (175C) on a deep-fry thermometer. At this temperature, a 1-inch cube of bread will turn golden brown in 65 seconds. Fry meatballs until browned on all sides, about 4 minutes. Remove from skillet and set aside. Drain all but 2 tablespoons oil from skillet. Stir in remaining ingredients. Bring to a simmer. Reduce heat. Add meatballs. Cover and cook over medium heat 30 minutes or until meatballs are firm. Serve hot. Spoon sauce over meatballs. Makes 6 meatballs.

☀ Ground-Meat Kebabs

Kefta Kabab (Morocco)

I watched Moroccans in Marrakech prepare delicious sausage-like burgers over a portable brazier.

1 lb. ground lean beef or lamb	*1 teaspoon paprika*
1/4 cup chopped fresh parsley	*1 teaspoon freshly ground*
1/4 cup chopped cilantro	*pepper*
1 medium onion, grated	*Salt to taste*
1 teaspoon ground cumin	

Combine all ingredients in a large bowl. Mix well. Let stand 1 hour to blend flavors. Preheat oven to broil. Or prepare hot coals on barbecue grill. Using about 1/4 cup mixture for each kebab, mold into a sausage shape around flat metal skewers. Moistening your hands will help mold the meat mixture onto skewers. Taper ends of sausage shapes to prevent meat from slipping off skewers during cooking. Place skewers on broiler rack 4 inches from heat source on grill or over hot coals. Turn frequently to brown evenly until meat is done as desired, 10 to 15 minutes. Makes 8 to 10 servings.

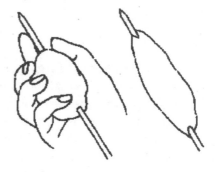

Picnic Meatballs
Kufteh Tabrizi (Iran)

Stuffed meatballs are festive fare for a picnic held on the 13th day of the Persian New Year.

2 tablespoons butter or
   margarine
1 medium onion, chopped
2 lbs. ground lean beef
4 eggs
1-1/2 cups garbanzo-bean flour
1 cup water
Salt and freshly ground pepper
   to taste
Pinch of saffron threads or
   powder

1/2 cup coarsely chopped
   walnuts
2 large hard-cooked eggs,
   coarsely chopped
10 pitted prunes
1/2 cup raisins or dried currants
4 cups Beef Broth, page 29,
   or water
Salt and freshly ground pepper
   to taste
Pinch of saffron threads or
   powder

Melt butter or margarine in a small skillet. Add onion. Sauté until onion is tender and golden brown. Set aside. Combine beef, eggs, bean flour, 1 cup water, salt, pepper and saffron in a large bowl. Mix well. Knead until meat mixture is dough-like. Pinch off pieces of meat mixture about 3 inches in diameter. Shape into large patties. Place 1 teaspoon walnuts, 1 teaspoon sautéed onion, 1 teaspoon chopped egg, 1 prune and 1 teaspoon raisins or currants in center of each patty. Mold patty around filling, pinching seams to enclose filling completely. Shape into meatballs. Place meatballs in a large shallow saucepan. Pour 4 cups broth or water over meatballs. Sprinkle with salt, pepper and saffron. Bring to a boil. Reduce heat and cover. Simmer over low heat 40 minutes or until meatballs are done as desired. Serve hot. Makes 10 large meatballs.

Garbanzo-bean flour, a high-protein flour, may be purchased at Middle Eastern grocery stores and some health-food stores. See page 15 for substitution information.

Fried Meatballs
Keftedes Tiganites (Greece)

Basic meatballs to serve on wooden picks as appetizers or with your favorite sauce over pasta or rice.

1 lb. ground lean lamb or beef
1 medium onion, finely chopped
1 garlic clove, minced
2 slices white bread, crusts
 removed
Water
1 egg, beaten
3 tablespoons chopped fresh
 parsley

1 tablespoon chopped fresh mint
 or 1 teaspoon crushed dried-
 leaf mint
2 or 3 tablespoons dry red wine
 or water
Pinch of ground allspice
Salt and freshly ground pepper
 to taste
All-purpose flour
Oil for frying

Combine meat, onion and garlic in a large bowl. Moisten bread in water. Squeeze dry. Add to meat mixture. Add egg, parsley, mint, wine or water, allspice, salt and pepper. Mix well. Refrigerate 1 hour to blend flavors. Pinch off pieces of meat mixture 1 inch in diameter. Shape into balls. Roll in flour. Pour oil 1/2 inch deep into a large skillet. Heat to 350F (175C) on a deep-fry thermometer. At this temperature, a 1-inch cube of bread will turn golden brown in 65 seconds. Carefully lower a few meatballs at a time into hot oil. Do not crowd in skillet. Fry until browned on all sides and done as desired. Drain on paper towels. Serve hot. Makes 18 to 20 meatballs.

꒡꒡꒡꒡꒡꒡꒡꒡꒡꒡꒡꒡꒡꒡꒡꒡꒡꒡꒡꒡꒡꒡꒡꒡꒡꒡꒡꒡꒡꒡꒡꒡꒡꒡꒡꒡

Beef & Onion Stew
Stifado (Greece)

If you like sauerbraten, you'll enjoy this sweet-and-sour stew.

1/4 cup olive oil
2 lbs. lean boneless beef chuck,
    cubed
1 lb. small white onions, peeled
5 garlic cloves, minced
1 teaspoon pickling spice, tied in
    cheesecloth
1 cinnamon stick

4 whole cloves
1/2 cup vinegar
1 (1-lb.) can whole tomatoes,
    drained
1/2 cup Beef Broth, page 29,
    or water
Salt and freshly ground pepper
    to taste

Heat olive oil in a large saucepan. Add beef. Cook until browned on all sides. Add onions and garlic. Cook until onions are golden. Add pickling spice in cheesecloth, cinnamon stick, cloves, vinegar, tomatoes, broth or water, salt and pepper. Bring to a boil. Reduce heat and cover. Simmer over low heat 1-1/2 to 2 hours or until meat is very tender. Remove pickling spice. Serve stew hot. Makes 6 to 8 servings.

Beef Curry
Kari (Iraq)

Curry probably came to Iraq from India while the British ruled both countries.

1/4 cup butter or margarine	2 cups water
4 large onions, chopped	2 lbs. lean beef or lamb, cut into
4 garlic cloves, minced	1-inch cubes
1/4 cup Madras curry powder	Salt and freshly ground pepper
or other Indian curry powder	to taste
6 medium tomatoes, diced	4 medium potatoes, diced
3 tablespoons tomato paste	Hot cooked rice, if desired

Melt butter or margarine in a large saucepan. Add onions and garlic. Sauté until golden but not browned. Stir in curry powder. Reduce heat. Cook over low heat 10 minutes to blend flavors. Add tomatoes. Sauté 3 minutes. Mix tomato paste with water. Stir into onion mixture. Add meat, salt and pepper. Bring to a boil. Reduce heat and cover. Simmer over low heat 1 hour. Add potatoes. Cook, covered, 40 minutes longer or until meat is tender. Serve over hot cooked rice, if desired. Makes 6 servings.

Variations
* Chicken Curry: Omit meat. Substitute 3 pounds chicken pieces. Cook 20 minutes before adding potatoes.
* Vegetarian Curry: Omit meat. Add potatoes after adding tomato-paste mixture and bringing to a boil. Cook 15 minutes. Add 2 pounds sliced summer squash, zucchini or green beans, or 1 medium, cubed eggplant, 2 cups green peas or 2 (10-ounce) packages drained, thawed, frozen okra. Other vegetables may be substituted.

Kubbe Filling

Use this tasty filling to make Stuffed Meatballs, page 87.

2 tablespoons olive oil
2 small onions, finely chopped
3/4 lb. coarsely ground lean beef

1/2 teaspoon Mixed Spice,
   page 139, or salt and freshly
   ground pepper to taste

Heat olive oil in a medium skillet. Add onions. Sauté until tender. Add beef. Cook until beef is browned and crumbly. Add Mixed Spice or salt and pepper. Cook 1 minute longer to blend flavors. Makes enough filling for Stuffed Meatballs.

Shish Kebab

Sis Kebabi (Turkey)

Vary your kebabs by adding small whole onions and sliced zucchini.

1 large onion
1/4 cup olive oil
1/2 cup red-wine vinegar
2 garlic cloves, minced
Salt and freshly ground black
   pepper to taste
1 (3-1/2- to 4-1/2-lb.) leg of
   lamb, boned, cut in
   1-1/2-inch cubes

1 large eggplant, cubed
4 medium tomatoes, quartered,
   or 16 cherry tomatoes
4 green bell peppers, halved or
   quartered
2 tablespoons butter or
   margarine, melted

Cut onion in half lengthwise, then slice to make long, thin strips. Combine olive oil, vinegar, onion strips, garlic, salt and black pepper in a large shallow bowl. Mix well. Add meat. Toss to coat well. Cover and marinate in refrigerator 2 to 24 hours. Preheat oven to broil. Or prepare hot coals on barbecue grill. Alternately thread marinated lamb, eggplant, tomatoes and green pepper on long metal skewers. Brush with butter or margarine. Place skewers on broiler rack 4 inches from heat source or on grill over hot coals. Cook, turning and basting frequently with marinade, until meat is done as desired, 15 to 20 minutes. Makes 8 servings.

Greek Stew
Yahni (Greece)

A hearty basic stew with many seasonal variations.

1/4 cup olive oil
2 medium onions, chopped
2 garlic cloves, minced
2 lbs. lean boneless lamb, cut in
   1-inch cubes
1 lb. medium tomatoes, chopped,
   or 1 (1-lb.) can whole
   tomatoes, drained, crushed

1 tablespoon chopped fresh
   parsley
Salt and freshly ground pepper
   to taste
2 cups Beef Broth, page 29,
   or water
Juice of 1/2 lemon (1-1/2
   tablespoons), if desired

Heat olive oil in a large saucepan. Add onions and garlic. Sauté until onions are tender. Add lamb. Cook until lamb is browned on all sides. Add tomatoes, parsley, salt and pepper. Cook 1 minute. Add broth or water. Bring to a boil. Reduce heat and cover. Simmer over low heat 1-1/2 to 2 hours or until meat is tender. Sprinkle with lemon juice before serving, if desired. Makes 6 servings.

Variations

✽ Lamb & Green-Bean Stew: Add 1 pound trimmed green beans, broken in 1-inch pieces, to stew 40 minutes before end of cooking time. Cover and cook as desired.

✽ Lamb & Artichoke Stew: Add 6 small artichokes, outer leaves and fuzzy chokes removed, to stew 30 minutes before end of cooking time. Cover and cook as directed.

✽ Lamb & Potato Stew: Add 2 large new potatoes, peeled and thickly sliced, to stew 40 minutes before end of cooking time. Cover and cook as directed.

꒰꒱꒰꒱꒰꒱꒰꒱꒰꒱꒰꒱꒰꒱꒰꒱꒰꒱꒰꒱꒰꒱꒰꒱꒰꒱꒰꒱꒰

Upside-Down Meat Pie

Makloubeh (Arabic)

The top rice layer ends up in the bottom of this delicately spiced stew.

1/4 cup vegetable oil
2 medium onions, chopped
1 garlic clove, minced
1/4 cup slivered almonds or pine nuts
1-1/2 lbs. boneless lean lamb, beef or veal, diced or coarsely chopped
1/4 teaspoon ground cumin
1/8 teaspoon ground allspice
Pinch of ground cinnamon
Pinch of ground cloves
Pinch of ground cardamom
Salt and freshly ground pepper to taste

About 1-1/2 cups Beef Broth, page 29, or water
1 small eggplant, unpeeled, cut lengthwise into 1/4-inch slices
Salt
Oil for frying
1 cup long-grain rice
Boiling water
1/4 cup warm water
1/4 teaspoon saffron threads or powder
Dash of rose water
Broth or water as needed

Heat 1/4 cup oil in a large saucepan. Add onions, garlic and almonds or pine nuts. Sauté until onions are tender. Add meat. Cook until meat is browned. Add cumin, allspice, cinnamon, cloves, cardamom, salt and pepper. Add 1-1/2 cups broth or water. Bring to a boil. Reduce heat and cover. Simmer over low heat 1 hour or until meat is tender. Sprinkle eggplant slices with salt. Let stand 5 minutes to leach out bitter flavor. Pat dry. Pour oil for frying 1/2 inch deep into a large skillet. Heat to 375F (190C) on a deep-fry thermometer. At this temperature, a 1-inch cube of bread will turn brown in 50 seconds. Fry eggplant slices, turning once, until golden on both sides. Drain on paper towels. Place rice in a medium bowl. Add boiling water to cover. Let stand 5 minutes. Pour 1/4 cup warm water into a small bowl. Sprinkle saffron over water. Add rose water. Drain rice. Return to medium bowl. Strain saffron mixture over rice. Discard saffron threads, if used. Toss rice mixture to mix well. Set aside. When meat is done, strain pan juices into a 2-cup measure. Add broth or water to make 1-1/2 cups. Set aside. Brush oil on bottom and side of a 10-inch skillet with rounded side. Spread meat evenly in skillet. Layer eggplant slices over meat. Spread rice over eggplant slices. Carefully pour reserved 1-1/2 cups broth mixture over rice. Cover and cook over medium heat 5 minutes. Reduce heat and cover. Simmer over low heat 30 minutes or until rice is tender and most of liquid is absorbed. Mixture should be moist but firm. Keep covered until ready to serve. Loosen edge of rice with a spatula. Place a platter upside-down on skillet. Invert skillet and platter. Remove skillet. Serve meat pie immediately. Makes 6 servings.

Roast Lamb with Potatoes
Arni Psito (Greece)

Greeks enjoy lamb well-done inside and crisp outside.

1 (4- to 5-lb.) leg of lamb
4 garlic cloves, slivered
3 tablespoons chopped fresh
    mint or 1 tablespoon crushed
    dried-leaf mint
Salt and freshly ground pepper
    to taste
1/2 cup water
6 medium potatoes, peeled,
    thinly sliced or quartered
Juice of 1/2 lemon
    (1-1/2 tablespoons)

Salt and freshly ground pepper
    to taste
2 tablespoons butter or
    margarine, diced
2 large onions, sliced, separated
    in rings
2 large tomatoes, chopped
1 bay leaf
1 cinnamon stick
About 1 cup Beef Broth,
    page 29, or water
1/2 cup dry red wine

Preheat oven to 350F (175C). Make slits in several places around surface of lamb. Insert slivers of garlic and mint leaves into slits or rub lamb with dried mint. Sprinkle with salt and pepper. Place lamb in roasting pan. Add 1/2 cup water to pan. Bake 1 hour. Place potatoes around lamb. Sprinkle with lemon juice, salt and pepper. Dot with butter or margarine. Scatter onion rings and tomatoes over lamb and potatoes. Place bay leaf and cinnamon stick on top of lamb. Add 1/2 cup broth or water and wine to pan. Bake, basting frequently with pan juices, 1-1/2 hours longer or until done as desired. Add remaining broth or water as needed to keep pan moist. Serve lamb with vegetables and pan juices. Makes 6 to 8 servings.

Roast Leg of Lamb with Orzo
Giouvetsi (Greece)

Use a baking dish that's pretty enough to serve from.

1 (5- to 6-lb.) leg of lamb	1 cup water
4 garlic cloves, slivered	Juice of 2 lemons (6 tablespoons)
1/4 cup fresh mint or	4 cups Chicken or Beef Broth,
2 tablespoons crushed	page 29
dried-leaf mint	2 cups orzo
1 teaspoon crushed dried-leaf	1/2 cup tomato sauce
oregano	Salt and freshly ground pepper
Salt and freshly ground pepper	to taste
to taste	1/2 cup grated Kefalotiri or
1 large onion, thinly sliced	Parmesan cheese

Preheat oven to 350F (175C). Rinse lamb and pat dry. Make deep slits in lamb in several places. Insert slivered garlic and fresh mint in slits. If using dried mint, combine with oregano, salt and pepper. Rub lamb all over with oregano mixture. Spread onion slices evenly in a large baking dish. Place lamb over onion slices. Pour water into baking dish. Bake 2-1/2 hours or until a meat thermometer inserted in thickest part of roast registers 160F (70C). Place roast on a platter. Sprinkle with lemon juice. Set aside and keep warm. Scrape up brown bits from baking dish. Skim off fat with a large spoon. Set aside baking dish with pan juices and brown bits. Pour broth into a large saucepan. Bring to a boil. Add orzo, tomato sauce, salt and pepper. Reduce heat. Cook, uncovered, over medium heat 20 minutes or until orzo is tender and most of the liquid is absorbed. Add cooked orzo to pan juices. Sprinkle with cheese. Toss to mix well. Bake 15 minutes longer. Carve lamb. Arrange slices over noodles. Makes 6 servings.

 # Grilled Spicy Calves' Liver
Boulfaf (Morocco)

An exciting blend of spices lifts lowly liver to noble heights. Try it also with chicken livers to serve as hot appetizers with drinks or as main course over rice.

1/4 cup peanut oil or olive oil	*Salt and freshly ground pepper*
2 teaspoons ground cumin	*to taste*
2 teaspoons paprika	*1 lb. calves' liver, cut in 1-inch*
1/2 teaspoon chili powder	*cubes*

   Preheat oven to broil. Or prepare hot coals on barbecue grill. Combine oil, cumin, paprika, chili powder, salt and pepper in a large bowl. Add liver. Toss to coat well. Marinate in refrigerator 1 hour or longer, tossing occasionally. Thread 4 or 5 liver cubes on each skewer. Place skewers on broiler rack 4 inches from heat source or on grill over hot coals. Cook, turning frequently to brown evenly, until livers are browned, about 10 minutes. Makes 6 servings.

Variations
✳ Kukurec *(Turkey)*: Use calves' liver in combination with any quick-cooking organ meats, such as hearts, kidneys or lung, cut into cubes or bite-size pieces. If desired, ask the butcher for some caul to wind around meats on skewers before cooking.

FISH, POULTRY & EGGS

Fish

Religious restrictions and cultural attitudes have limited the use of seafood in the Middle East. Judaic dietary laws prohibit eating any seafood without scales or fins. All crustaceans, such as shrimp, lobster and crab, are taboo. Islamic law allows fish and shellfish in the diet, but restrictions are often imposed by custom. A Bedouin from the inland desert of Saudi Arabia has probably never eaten fish nor observed it being served.

Still, fish dishes abound in the Middle East because many countries are surrounded, patched or veined by waterways. The Tigris and Euphrates Rivers supply numerous varieties of fish. Masgoof, a large fish of the flounder family is sold by the foot at stalls along the Tigris River banks in Baghdad and cooked threaded on eucalyptus branches over an open circular fire.

Waters of the Aegean Sea, the Mediterranean Sea, the Sea of Marmara, the Black Sea, the Caspian Sea and the Red Sea are filled with swordfish, turbot, mussels, shrimp and crab. Turkey's Bosphorus strait supplies firm-fleshed sea bass called *levrek* and a turbot known as *kalkan*. These are sold from fishing boats along the Galata Bridge in Istanbul.

Grey mullet from the Red Sea produces the expensive roe which are dried to serve as hors d'oeuvre on toast at Egypt's finest tables. Carp, raised in salt-water ponds in Israel, replaces pike commonly used in gefilte fish. Greeks, the lovers of the seas that surround them, are superb fish cooks. One of the most dramatically fragrant fish is baked plaki-style, meaning filled with herbs and vegetables. Stuffed mussels are relished by Armenians, Turks and Greeks. See Rice-Stuffed Mussels on page 109.

Poultry

There was a time when a scrawny chicken stewing in a pot was considered sheer luxury. Today poultry production in the Middle East is on the rise and exports from the around the world keep chicken high in use and popularity. In Baghdad, stalls sell what Iraqis call *kentak-ee*, a form of the word *Kentucky* after the popular take-out brand in the United States. In Jordan, Chicken Sumac is a common vendors' offering.

The Persian cuisine is especially rich in poultry dishes. The sweet flesh lends itself to the exotic treatment with herbs, fruits and candied fruits. Dishes classified as stews served with rice, or *khoresht*, include a fabulous Duckling in Walnut-Pomegranate Sauce, adored by most Persians.

North African cooks prepare Lemon Chicken using pickled lemon and olives to fill *bastela* or bake chicken tajine-style in a cone-shaped ceramic utensil.

Eggs

In Middle Eastern cooking terms eggs are used both to accompany other foods and as a main dish for breakfast, lunch or dinner. You will find omelets, called *kuku* in the Persian cuisine, made with a riot of herbs that might shock. Tunisians prepare baked whole eggs in filo-dough packages for breakfast and Greeks love scrambled eggs with feta cheese. Likewise Armenians enjoy mixing pieces of pastrami with scrambled eggs. Cured beef, called *basterma*, is found at most Middle Eastern grocery stores. Prosciutto or jerky can be substituted. You will recognize it by the pungent ground fenugreek coating used in many curry blends.

MENU

Persian Carpet Dinner

Mixed-Herb Plate,
page 28

Duckling in Walnut-
Pomegranate Sauce,
page 106

Persian Steamed Rice,
page 71

Persian Almond Rolls,
page 126

Tea

Chicken Sumac
Musakhan (Jordan)

Use only sumac purchased at Middle-Eastern grocery stores. Many species are not related to the spice.

1 (2-1/2-lb.) chicken, quartered	*4 Arabic pocket breads*
Chicken Broth, page 29, or	*1/4 cup olive oil*
water	*4 medium onions, chopped, or*
1 small celery stalk with leaves	*sliced and separated in rings*
1 small onion, halved	*4 teaspoons sumac*
Salt and freshly ground pepper	*1/4 cup or more toasted pine*
to taste	*nuts, page 46*

Place chicken quarters in a large saucepan. Add broth or water barely to cover. Add celery, onion halves, salt and pepper. Bring to a boil. Reduce heat and cover. Simmer over low heat 30 minutes. Remove chicken. Reserve 1/3 cup broth. Preheat oven to 350F (175C). Place Arabic pocket breads on an ungreased baking sheet with rimmed sides. Set aside. Heat olive oil in a large skillet. Add chopped onions. Sauté until onions are browned, about 8 minutes. Spread onions equally over each pocket bread. Top each onion-covered bread with a cooked chicken quarter. Pour reserved broth over chicken quarters. Sprinkle each chicken quarter with 1 teaspoon sumac. Bake 30 minutes or until chicken quarters are golden brown. Garnish with pine nuts. Makes 4 servings.

Variations

✳ Cut chicken into small pieces. Place on bread. Spread onions over chicken. Top with pine nuts.

✳ Bread made with refrigerator biscuits, crescent-roll dough or thawed frozen dough may be used in place of pocket bread. Pat dough for biscuits or rolls or thawed dough into 6- to 8-inch circles. Bake at 350F (175C) 10 minutes to set. Use as directed above.

՜՜՜՜՜՜՜՜՜՜՜՜՜՜՜՜՜՜՜՜՜՜՜՜՜՜՜՜՜՜՜

Oasis Duck

Bat el Fayyoumi (Egypt)

Ducks raised in the Oasis of Fayyoum in Egypt are prepared this way.

1 (3- to 3-1/2-lb.) duckling,
    cleaned
Salt and freshly ground pepper
    to taste
Juice of 1 lemon (3 tablespoons)
1/2 cup coarse-grade bulgur
Water
2 tablespoons butter or
    margarine
1 medium onion, finely chopped

1 small heart of celery with
    leaves, chopped
1 garlic clove, minced
1 small onion, chopped
1/4 cup lemon juice
1 teaspoon salt
1 tablespoon chopped fresh dill
    or 1 teaspoon dill weed, if
    desired
1/2 cup water

Rinse duckling thoroughly. Sprinkle all over and inside cavities with salt and pepper. Rub with 3 tablespoons lemon juice. Refrigerate. Place bulgur in a medium bowl. Add water to cover. Let stand about 20 minutes or until water is absorbed. Use your hands to squeeze out any excess water. Fluff to separate grains. Preheat oven to 350F (175C). Melt butter or margarine in a large skillet. Add onion, celery and garlic. Sauté until onion is tender. Add softened bulgur, salt and pepper. Mix well. Stuff into duckling cavity, packing loosely. Close cavity opening with metal or bamboo skewers. In a small bowl, combine onion, 1/4 cup lemon juice and salt. Mix well. Rub all over duckling. Sprinkle with dill, if desired. Bake 2 hours, basting frequently with pan juices. Add 1/2 cup water to pan juices as they evaporate. Makes 4 servings.

Chicken & Rice Skillet

Kabsa (Arab Gulf States)

This colorful party dish is probably a forerunner of paella.

1/4 cup butter or margarine
1 (2-1/2- to 3-lb.) chicken,
    cut up
1 large onion, chopped
5 garlic cloves, minced
1/4 cup tomato sauce or puree
2 medium tomatoes, chopped
2 medium carrots, grated
Grated peel of 1 orange
3 whole cloves
2 cardamom pods or
    1/2 teaspoon ground
    cardamom seeds

1 cinnamon stick
Salt and freshly ground pepper
    to taste
3 cups Chicken Broth,
    page 29
1 cup long-grain rice
1/4 cup raisins
1/4 cup toasted sliced or slivered
    almonds, page 46

Melt butter or margarine in a large skillet. Add chicken pieces. Sauté until browned on all sides. Remove from skillet. Set aside. Add onion and garlic to skillet. Sauté until onion is tender. Stir in tomato sauce or puree. Simmer over low heat 1 minute to blend flavors. Add tomatoes, carrots, orange peel, cloves, cardamom, cinnamon stick, salt and pepper. Cook 1 minute. Add broth. Return chicken pieces to skillet. Bring to a boil. Reduce heat and cover. Simmer over low heat 30 minutes. Stir rice into liquid between pieces of chicken. Or remove chicken, stir in rice, then return chicken pieces to skillet. Cover. Simmer 30 minutes longer or until rice is tender. Garnish with raisins and almonds. Makes 6 to 8 servings.

Lemon Chicken
Poulet au Citron (Morocco)

This dish is a favorite of Moroccans everywhere.

2 (2-lb.) chickens
2 cups Chicken Broth,
    page 29, or water
1/4 cup peanut oil
1 tablespoon olive oil
2 medium onions, sliced
Gizzards from 1 chicken
1 garlic clove, minced
1 teaspoon ground ginger or
    1 (1-inch) piece fresh
    ginger root

Pinch of crushed saffron threads
    or powder
Salt and freshly ground pepper
    to taste
Peel of 1 Preserved Lemon,
    page 137, or 1 fresh lemon,
    quartered
1/2 cup green olives
Lemon wedges for garnish
Parsley sprigs for garnish

Rinse chickens thoroughly. Place in a large pot. Add broth or water. Pour peanut oil and olive oil over chickens. Add onions, gizzards, garlic, ginger, saffron, salt and pepper. Bring to a boil. Reduce heat and cover. Simmer over low heat 40 minutes or until chickens are almost tender, turning once or twice to cook evenly. Discard gizzards and fresh ginger, if used. Add lemon peel or fresh lemon. Simmer 15 minutes longer or until chickens are tender. Discard lemon peel or fresh lemon. Add olives. Heat through. Garnish with lemon wedges and parsley. Makes 6 to 8 servings.

Duckling in Walnut-Pomegranate Sauce

Fesenjan (Iran)

Celebrate with this party dish during the winter holidays when pomegranates are in season.

1/4 cup butter or margarine
1 large onion, finely chopped
1 (4-lb.) duckling, cleaned
2-1/2 cups Chicken Broth,
*   page 29*
Juice of 1 lemon (3 tablespoons)
Salt and freshly ground pepper
*   to taste*

1/2 cup pomegranate juice
2 cups ground walnuts
*   (about 10 oz.)*
1 tablespoon sugar
Pomegranate seeds for garnish
Walnut halves for garnish

Melt butter or margarine in a large pot. Add onion. Sauté until tender. Rinse duckling thoroughly. Add to onion in pot. Cook until browned on all sides, about 10 minutes. Add broth, lemon juice, salt and pepper. Bring to a boil. Reduce heat and cover. Simmer over low heat 40 minutes or until duckling is barely tender. Remove duckling from pot. Set aside. Skim excess fat from pan juices. Stir in pomegranate juice, ground walnuts and sugar. Return duckling to pot. Bring to a boil. Reduce heat and cover. Simmer over low heat 1 hour, stirring sauce occasionally to prevent sticking. Place duckling on a platter. Spoon sauce over duckling. Garnish with pomegranate seeds and walnut halves. Makes 3 or 4 servings.

If pomegranates are unavailable, substitute pomegranate molasses, which may be purchased at Middle Eastern grocery stores, or grenadine syrup, also available at supermarkets.

Fish Bake
Psari Plaki (Greece)

Plaki means *cooked with herbs and vegetables.* The result is irresistibly aromatic.

1 (2-1/2- to 3-lb.) whole fish such as white fish, sea bass, perch or other firm-flesh fish, dressed
Juice of 1 lemon (3 tablespoons)
Salt and freshly ground white pepper to taste
3 large onions
1/2 cup olive oil
2 garlic cloves, minced
5 medium carrots, peeled, sliced diagonally
5 medium celery stalks, sliced diagonally

1 (8-oz.) can tomato sauce
1/2 tomato-sauce can dry red or white wine
1 tablespoon chopped fresh parsley
1 tablespoon chopped fresh dill or 1 teaspoon dill weed
Salt and freshly ground black pepper to taste
1 medium lemon, thinly sliced
1 (1-lb.) can whole tomatoes, drained, or 4 fresh tomatoes

Rinse fish. Pat dry. Sprinkle fish all over and inside cavity with lemon juice. Sprinkle lightly with salt and white pepper. Set aside. Cut onions in half lengthwise, then slice to make long, thin strips. Set aside. Preheat oven to 350F (175C). Heat olive oil in a large skillet. Add garlic, onion strips, carrots and celery. Sauté until vegetables are tender but not browned. Add tomato sauce, wine, parsley, dill, salt and black pepper. Bring to a boil. Reduce heat. Cook over medium heat 3 minutes. Place fish in a large baking pan or casserole. Spoon some of the vegetables into fish cavity. Spread remaining vegetables with liquid on and around fish. Overlap lemon slices across fish. Crush or chop canned tomatoes or dice fresh tomatoes. Spread over fish and vegetables. Cover and bake 1-1/4 to 1-1/2 hours or until fish flakes easily when pierced with a fork. Makes 6 to 8 servings.

Shrimp Abu Dhabi
Murabyan (Arab Gulf States)

Pink Gulf shrimp are prepared simply and served plain or
with rice.

1 lb. large shrimp or prawns
(about 12)
Salt to taste
1/2 cup all-purpose flour
2 tablespoons butter or
margarine

2 tablespoons olive oil
1 large onion, chopped
2 garlic cloves, minced
2 tablespoons chopped cilantro
Juice of 1 lime (3 tablespoons)
Cilantro sprigs for garnish

Clean and devein shrimp or prawns, removing shells but leaving
shells on tails intact. Sprinkle shrimp or prawns with salt. Roll
lightly in flour, shaking off excess. Melt butter or margarine
with olive oil in a large skillet. Add onion and garlic. Sauté
until onion is tender. Add shrimp or prawns and
chopped cilantro. Sauté until shrimp or prawns
are golden, about 7 minutes. Place on a platter.
Sprinkle with lime juice. Garnish with cilantro
sprigs. Makes 4 servings.

꜒꜖꜒꜖꜒꜖꜒꜖꜒꜖꜒꜖꜒꜖꜒꜖꜒꜖꜒꜖꜒꜖꜒꜖꜒꜖꜒꜖꜒꜖꜒꜖꜒꜖꜒꜖

Rice-Stuffed Mussels

Midye Dolmasi (Turkey)

Stuffed mussels or clams are enjoyed as an appetizer or a main dish.

*6 dozen mussels or clams in
   the shell*
1/2 cup olive oil
2 medium onions, chopped
2 cups short-grain rice
1/4 cup raisins
1/4 cup pine nuts
1/4 teaspoon ground cinnamon
1/4 teaspoon ground allspice

*Salt and freshly ground pepper
   to taste*
1 cup bottled clam liquor
*1 cup Chicken Broth,
   page 29, or water*
*2 cups Chicken Broth,
   page 29, or water*
Lemon wedges

Scrub mussel or clam shells thoroughly with a stiff brush to remove hairy tufts. Discard any already opened shells. This indicates they are not safe to eat. To open scrubbed shells for stuffing and cooking, freeze a few minutes until shells open; or pry open with a clam opener; or dip in warm (150F, 65C) water 2 to 3 minutes, depending on thickness of the shell. Discard any shells that are dry inside and any with an offensive odor. Rinse thoroughly in cool water. Heat olive oil in a large skillet. Add onions. Sauté until tender. Add rice, raisins, pine nuts, cinnamon, allspice, salt and pepper. Sauté until rice is glazed. Add clam liquor and 1 cup broth or water.

Bring to a boil. Reduce heat and cover. Cook over medium-low heat 10 minutes or until liquid is absorbed. Spoon 1 tablespoon rice mixture into each mussel or clam. Close shell. Wind string several times around each shell to secure. Tie tightly. Place in a large casserole or Dutch oven with lid. Add 2 cups broth or water. Bring to a boil. Reduce heat and cover. Cook over medium-low heat 20 to 25 minutes or until rice is tender. Remove from heat and uncover. Let mussels or clams stand in pan juices until cool enough to handle. Arrange on a large platter. Untie or snip off strings to open shells. Serve with lemon wedges. Makes 6 to 8 servings.

Shrimp & Feta Bake
Garides Giouvetsi (Greece)

As a first course or a main dish, this flavorful seafood from the Greek islands is memorable.

1 lb. large shrimp or prawns
   (about 12)
1/4 cup olive oil
1 small yellow onion, minced
2 green onions, chopped
2 garlic cloves, minced
2 large tomatoes, diced
1/4 cup dry white wine
2 tablespoons chopped fresh
   parsley

1 teaspoon crushed dried-leaf
   oregano
Salt and freshly ground pepper
   to taste
1/4 cup crumbled feta cheese
   (1 oz.)
Chopped parsley for garnish

Clean and devein shrimp or prawns, removing shells but leaving shells on tails intact. Refrigerate. Heat olive oil in a large skillet. Add yellow onion, green onions and garlic. Sauté until onions are tender. Add tomatoes, wine, 2 tablespoons chopped parsley, oregano, salt and pepper. Cook over medium heat 30 minutes or until sauce thickens. Preheat oven to 350F (175C). Spoon half the tomato sauce into a medium casserole. Cover with shrimp or prawns. Top with remaining sauce. Sprinkle cheese evenly over sauce. Bake 15 to 20 minutes or until shrimp is pink and cheese is golden brown and slightly melted. Garnish with parsley. Makes 4 servings.

Vinegared Fish Kebabs
Kilic Sis (Turkey)

The same marinade can be used on lamb chops.

1/4 cup vinegar or onion juice	1-1/2 lbs. swordfish or other
1/2 teaspoon salt	firm-flesh fish fillets
1 tablespoon olive oil	8 wood skewers
1 tablespoon chopped thyme	Parsley sprigs
leaves	8 lemon wedges

Preheat oven to broil. Or prepare hot coals on barbecue grill. Combine vinegar or onion juice, salt, olive oil and thyme leaves in a medium bowl. Cut fish into large cubes. Place in bowl and toss to coat well with vinegar mixture. Thread fish on skewers. Place fish on broiler rack 4 inches from heat source or on grill over medium-low coals. Cook 4 minutes on each side, or until done. Cooking time will depend on type and thickness of fish. Serve on plate with parsley sprigs and lemon wedges. Makes 8 servings.

To extract juice from onion, grate onion and let stand in bowl with salt 10 minutes. Squeeze onion mixture with hands or a press.

꯹꯹꯹꯹꯹꯹꯹꯹꯹꯹꯹꯹꯹꯹꯹꯹꯹꯹꯹꯹꯹꯹꯹꯹꯹꯹꯹꯹꯹꯹꯹꯹꯹꯹꯹꯹

Eggs in a Package
La Breik à l'Oeuf (Tunisia)

Surprise your family with neat packages of eggs in filo for breakfast, lunch or a light supper.

1/2 cup chopped onion
1/4 cup chopped cilantro
6 filo pastry sheets
6 eggs

Salt and freshly ground pepper
  to taste
Paprika to taste
Oil for frying

Combine onion and cilantro in a small bowl. Place 1 filo sheet on a clean flat surface. Cover remining filo sheets with plastic wrap to prevent drying. Fold filo sheet into thirds lengthwise, making a long rectangle. Break 1 egg onto center of rectangle. Sprinkle with 2 tablespoons onion-cilantro mixture, salt, pepper and paprika. Fold filo over egg envelope-fashion, enclosing egg. Moisten seams with water and press lightly with your fingers to seal. Pierce in several places with a wooden pick to let steam escape while frying. Working with 1 filo sheet at a time, repeat with remaining filo sheets and eggs. Pour oil 1 inch deep into a large skillet. Heat to 350F (175C) on a deep-fry thermometer. At this temperature, a 1-inch cube of bread will turn golden brown in 65 seconds. Carefully lower each egg package into hot oil. Fry, turning frequently to cook evenly, until golden on both sides, 1 to 2 minutes. Serve hot. Remove from hot oil with a slotted spoon. Drain on paper towels. Makes 6 servings.

Variations
✳ Egg & Cheese in a Package: Add 1/4 cup crumbled feta cheese (about 1 ounce) or cottage cheese (about 2 ounces) to onion-cilantro mixture.

✳ Egg & Vegetables in a Package: Add 1/2 cup any diced cooked vegetable to onion-cilantro mixture.

✳ Ham & Egg in a Package: Add 1/4 cup chopped ham to onion-cilantro mixture.

Herb & Nut Omelet

Kuku Sabzi (Iran)

Expect a flavor surprise when you bite into this exotic omelet.

2 tablespoons butter or
   margarine
4 green onions, finely chopped
1 or 2 lettuce leaves, chopped
1/4 cup chopped fresh dill or
   2 tablespoons dill weed
1/2 cup chopped fresh parsley
1/4 cup chopped cilantro
2 tablespoons butter or
   margarine

8 eggs
1/2 teaspoon baking soda
1/2 teaspoon crushed saffron
   threads or saffron powder
1/8 teaspoon ground cinnamon
Salt and freshly ground pepper
   to taste
3 tablespoons chopped walnuts
3 tablespoons raisins

Preheat oven to 350F (175C). Melt 2 tablespoons butter or margarine in a large skillet with an ovenproof handle. Add green onions, lettuce, dill, parsley and cilantro. Sauté until onion is tender. Add 2 tablespoons butter or margarine. Heat until melted. In a medium bowl, combine eggs, baking soda, saffron, cinnamon, salt and pepper. Stir in walnuts and raisins. Add to herb mixture in skillet. Do not stir. Cook over medium heat until set around edges. Place in oven. Bake 20 to 30 minutes or until golden and set. Cut into wedges and serve immediately. Makes 6 to 8 servings.

Skillet Eggs & Meat
Kiymali Yumurta (Turkey)

A quick and simple dish to serve on busy days.

2 tablespoons butter or
  margarine
1 small onion, minced
1 pound ground lean beef or
  lamb
1 tablespoon chopped fresh
  parsley

1 tablespoon tomato paste
1/4 cup water
Salt and freshly ground pepper
  to taste
6 eggs
Paprika to taste

Melt butter or margarine in large skillet. Add onion. Sauté until onion is tender. Add ground beef or lamb. Cook until meat is crumbly and browned. Stir in parsley, tomato paste, water, salt and pepper. Mix well. Cover and simmer over low heat 10 minutes. Break eggs over meat mixture, spacing evenly around skillet. Cover and simmer over low heat 4 minutes or until eggs are done as desired. Sprinkle eggs with paprika. Makes 6 servings.

Pastrami With Eggs
Abukhd Havgitov (Armenia)

Turks and Armenians enjoy this common breakfast or luncheon dish using dried beef, called *basterma*.

2 tablespoons butter or
  margarine
1/2 lb. basterma or prosciutto,
  thinly sliced

6 eggs
Salt and freshly ground pepper
  to taste

Melt butter or margarine in a large skillet over low heat. Arrange basterma or prosciutto in a single layer in skillet. Cook over low heat until browned. Break eggs into skillet over meat. Cook until eggs are set. If desired, cover pan a few minutes to steam eggs. Makes 6 servings.

Variation

✳ Feta with Eggs: Omit basterma. Mix eggs with 2 cups crumbled feta cheese. Then cook until scrambled.

DESSERTS, PRESERVES
& CONFECTIONS

Desserts

The Byzantine and Ottoman taste for sweets has set the tone for ultra-rich desserts throughout the Mideast-Mediterranean areas. Perhaps the best-known category of desserts are pastries made with filo dough. These probably date back to Byzantine times. Nut-filled filo pastries are generally classified as *baklavas*. There is no end to the variety of their shapes and sizes, fillings and flavors. Syrians make baklava filled with pistachio nuts, shaping nut-filled rolls into nests. Armenians have a weakness for crinkled rolls called *burma*. A long dowel is required to make them. Other baklavas are rolled like cigarettes, folded into triangles, stacked or coiled.

Most are steeped in a medium simple syrup made with honey or sugar and flavored with lemon or other spices such as cardamom or nutmeg. The general rule is to add cooled syrup to hot pastry or hot syrup to cooled pastry to prevent syrup from crystallizing and to keep filo from becoming soggy. Fillings can vary according to the imagination. In Greece, a cream-filled filo pastry is known as *galaktoboureko* and in Tunisia almond paste or marzipan is the filling for cigarette-shape pastries.

Filo pastries keep well at room temperature for days, even weeks, although I do not recommend prolonged storage. Because baklavas are so rich, small portions go a long way. A single large pan, using 1 pound of filo and 1 pound of nuts, makes 40 or more pieces, making it an ideal and economic dessert for large parties.

Of all the cookies common to all cuisines in the Middle East, Wedding Cakes, known as *kourabiedes* in Greek, *kurabiye* in Turkish and *graybeh* in Arabic take first place. Each country has its own flavor version. In the Arab world, cardamom is a common flavoring. Greeks use cloves. Sponge cakes steeped in syrup are also a Middle Eastern tradition.

Creams, such as rice pudding, crème caramel, custards and cornstarch pudding known in the West as *blanc mange,* also are popular. Each region boasts a preferred flavoring touch. In Greece, cinnamon or cloves, pomegranates and almonds are preferred. Arabs prefer cardamom, orange-blossom or rose waters to flavor creams.

Preserves & Confections

Perhaps the most notable of all Middle Eastern preserves is milk which has gone through a fermentation process. *Yogurt* in Turkish, or *laban* in Arabic, probably originated long before any reference to its presence appears in recorded history. Trade, war, domination and travel probably spread yogurt throughout the Middle East. Immigrants brought it to the Western world where it now enjoys a glamorous and healthful image.

The recipe for Homemade Yogurt gives several methods. Failure occurs if the yogurt starter is faulty or the directions for arriving at the correct temperature are not followed. Yogurt made with nonfat or low-fat milk will not be as rich as yogurt made with whole milk or cream, but it is just as healthful.

Pickles, another major category of preserves and jams and fruit preserves make fine gifts. Marinated Greek Olives are easy to make using already cured olives. If you want to cure your own olives, consult your local Cooperative Extension Agent for guidance (in the U.S.). Home curing of olives can pose safety problems.

Middle East confections are distinguished for their extra sweetness. If you like sweets, you will undoubtedly enjoy Turkish Delight and Sesame Candy.

MENU

Dessert Party

Date Domes, page 118

Pistachio Baklava, pages 121, 122

Walnut Cake, pages 122, 123

Wedding Cakes, page 125

Minted Tea

Turkish Coffee

Date Domes
Ma'amul (Arabic)

Festive cookies are shaped in a special wooden mold called a *tabi*.

Date Filling, see below
1 cup unsalted butter or
    margarine, room temperature
1-1/2 cups granulated sugar
1-1/2 teaspoons brandy
1-1/2 teaspoons orange-blossom
    water
1 egg
1/2 teaspoon ground black-
    cherry kernels (mahlab),
    if desired

3 cups all-purpose flour
1 cup fine-grade semolina
Dash of salt
Powdered sugar for sprinkling

Date Filling:
1/2 lb. pitted dates
1 tablespoon butter or
    margarine, room temperature
1 teaspoon orange-blossom
    water, if desired

Prepare Date Filling. Set aside. Butter baking sheets. Set aside. Preheat oven to 350F (175C). Combine butter or margarine and granulated sugar in a large bowl. Cream until light and fluffy. Stir in brandy and orange-blossom water. Beat in egg. Add cherry kernels, if desired. Gradually add flour, semolina and salt until dough pulls away from side of bowl. Knead until smooth, about 5 minutes. Pinch off pieces of dough 1-1/2 inches in diameter. Shape into balls. Pat into 3-inch circles. Place 1 tablespoon date mixture in center of a circle. Pull edges of circle over filling and pinch together to enclose filling. Place cookie in decorative mold, or *tabi*. Pat down gently in mold. Knock molded cookie out of mold dome-side up onto greased baking sheet. Repeat with remaining dough circles and filling. Bake 20 minutes or until bottom of cookies are pale-golden. Do not let tops

of cookies brown. Cool on a rack. Sprinkle with powdered sugar while still warm. Makes 16 to 20 cookies.

Date Filling:
Cut up dates. Place in food processor or blender. Process to a paste. Add butter or margarine. Add orange-blossom water, if desired. Process until blended.

The tabi, *a dome-shaped mold with a handle, is generally available at Middle Eastern grocery stores. If no mold is available, use your hands to shape filled dough into balls, patties or bars.*

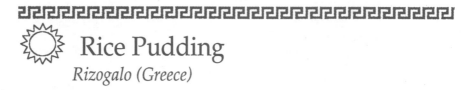

Rice Pudding
Rizogalo (Greece)

A creamy pudding to serve from a pretty bowl or in your most-delicate dessert dishes.

4 cups milk (1 qt.)
3 cups water
3/4 cup short-grain rice
1 cup sugar
2 or 3 egg yolks

1/2 cup milk
1 teaspoon vanilla extract or almond extract
Ground cinnamon for sprinkling

In a large saucepan, combine 4 cups milk, water and rice. Bring to a boil over medium heat. Reduce heat. Simmer, uncovered, over low heat until rice is soft and mixture is slightly thickened. Add sugar. Simmer over medium-low heat 5 minutes. In a small bowl, slightly beat egg yolks. Beat in 1/2 cup milk. Stir in a small amount of hot rice mixture into yolk mixture. Add yolk mixture to rice mixture in saucepan. Stir over low heat until blended. Stir in extract. Pour into custard cups or dessert bowls or a large serving bowl. Pudding will be thin but will thicken as it cools. Garnish with a sprinkle of cinnamon. Refrigerate several hours. Makes 6 to 12 servings.

Variation
✳ Egyptian Rice Pudding *(Roz bi-Laban):* Substitute 1 teaspoon rose water for extract. Garnish with chopped toasted almonds, page 46.

Shredded-Pastry Dessert

Kataifi (Greece)

Easy-to-use shredded filo, or *kadaif*, is usually available at Middle Eastern grocery stores.

Medium Syrup, page 134
2 cups coarsely chopped
   walnuts (about 10 oz.)
1 teaspoon ground cinnamon
1/4 teaspoon ground cloves

1 lb. fresh or thawed frozen
   shredded filo dough
1/2 cup unsalted butter,
   clarified, page 129, or
   margarine, melted

Prepare Medium Syrup. Set aside to cool. In a small bowl, combine walnuts, cinnamon and cloves. Set aside. Preheat oven to 350F (175C). Butter a 13" x 9" baking pan. Set aside. Separate shredded dough to loosen and fluff. Spread a third of the shredded dough in prepared baking pan. Sprinkle with a third of the clarified butter or melted margarine. Spread a third of the walnut mixture over dough. Spread with half the remaining shredded dough. Sprinkle with half the remaining butter or margarine. Sprinkle with remaining walnut mixture. Top with remaining shredded dough. Sprinkle with remaining butter or margarine. Bake 30 to 40 minutes or until golden brown. Pour half the cooled syrup over pastry. Let stand 10 minutes. Pour remaining syrup over pastry. Cut into 2-inch diamond or square shapes without removing from pan. Let stand 1 to 8 hours before serving. Makes 24 pieces.

Variations

✳ Shredded-Pastry Rolls: Pull off a 4" x 2" piece of shredded dough. Place flat, fluffing to loosen dough. Place 1 tablespoon nut mixture at bottom of rectangle. Roll up jelly-roll fashion, tucking in sides. Place roll in a buttered baking pan. Sprinkle with butter or margarine. Repeat with remaining shredded filo, nut mixture and butter or margarine. Bake at 350F (175C) 20 to 30 minutes or until rolls are golden. Add syrup as directed above. Makes 20 to 25 pieces.

✳ Arabic Cheese-Filled Pastry: Substitute the following cheese filling for the walnut filling: Combine 3/4 pound ricotta cheese, 1/4 cup sugar and 1 teaspoon orange-blossom water in a small bowl. Mix well.

☼ Christmas Pudding
Anushabur (Armenia)

This festive dessert is prepared in huge batches for large gatherings during the holidays.

1 cup fine- to medium-grade bulgur	2 cups sugar
Water	1 teaspoon rose water
12 cups water (3 qts.)	Ground cinnamon for garnish
1-1/2 cups golden raisins	Blanched almonds for garnish
2 cups dried apricots	Candied cherries for garnish

Place bulgur in a large saucepan. Add water to cover. Drain in a fine sieve. Discard water. Pour 12 cups water into saucepan. Add drained bulgur. Stir well. Bring to a boil. Remove from heat. Let stand 1 to 2 hours. Again, bring to a boil. Reduce heat and cover. Simmer over very low heat, stirring frequently to prevent sticking, 1-1/2 hours or until thickened. Fold in raisins, apricots and sugar. Cover. Simmer over very low heat 30 minutes longer, stirring frequently. Remove from heat. Add rose water. Turn pudding into a serving bowl. Refrigerate to chill. Sprinkle with cinnamon or decorate with almonds and cherries. Makes about 20 servings.

☼ Pistachio Baklava
Swareh (Syria/Lebanon)

This version of individual baklava is shaped like a rosette.

Medium Syrup, page 134	*1/2 cup unsalted butter,*
15 filo pastry sheets	*clarified, page 129, or*
2 cups coarsely chopped	*margarine, melted*
walnuts (about 10 oz.)	*2 cups coarsely chopped*
	pistachio nuts (about 1/2 lb.)

Prepare Medium Syrup. Set aside to cool. Preheat oven to 325F (165C). Stack filo pastry sheets. Cut through center to make 2 stacks. Stack again. Trim to measure 15 inches on the 2 long sides. Working with 1 filo sheet at a time, place on a flat surface. Cover remaining filo sheets with plastic wrap to prevent drying out. Spoon about 1 tablespoon walnuts 3 inches from bottom of filo to within 1/2 inch of edges. Fold in edges. Fold bottom over walnuts. Roll up tightly jelly-roll fashion. Coil the roll, using your thumb as a guide. Coil should be about 3 inches in diameter. Place on an ungreased baking sheet. Brush top with sides of coil with clarified butter or melted margarine. Repeat with remaining filo, nuts and butter or margarine. Bake 45 to 50 minutes or until golden. Pour cooled syrup over warm pastries. Let stand 1 hour. Spoon 1 tablespoon pistachio nuts into center of each coil. Tap nuts lightly to secure them to pastry. Makes 30 pastries.

Walnut Cake
Karitopita (Greece)

My friend Ann Pappas kindly shared her mother's recipe for this holiday cake.

Cinnamon Syrup, see below
7 eggs, separated
1-1/2 cups powdered sugar
1/4 cup all-purpose flour
1/2 teaspoon ground cinnamon
1/2 teaspoon ground cloves
1/2 teaspoon ground nutmeg
1/4 teaspoon baking soda
2 cups finely chopped walnuts
    (10 oz.)

6 Zwieback crackers, crushed, or
    1-1/2 cups crushed Zwieback
    or graham-cracker crumbs
2 tablespoons Cognac or brandy

Cinnamon Syrup:
1-1/2 cups sugar
3/4 cup water
1 cinnamon stick
5 whole cloves
1 lemon slice

Prepare Cinnamon Syrup. Set aside. Preheat oven to 350F (175C). Grease and flour a 9-inch square pan. Set aside. In a large bowl, beat egg yolks and powdered sugar until light and fluffy. Into a medium bowl, sift together flour, cinnamon, cloves, nutmeg and baking soda. Add nuts and cracker crumbs. Mix well. Gradually beat crumb mixture into egg mixture until blended. Add Cognac or brandy. Beat egg whites until stiff but not dry. Fold into cake batter. Pour into prepared pan. Bake 35 to 40 minutes or until a wooden pick inserted in center of cake comes out clean. Pour cooled syrup over warm cake. Let soak 20 minutes. Cut into 2-1/4-inch diamond or square shapes. Makes 16 servings.

Cinnamon Syrup:
Combine all ingredients in a medium saucepan. Bring to a boil. Boil until candy thermometer registers 212F (100C) or until a thin syrup is formed. Cool before pouring over warm cake. Or pour hot over cooled cake.

Sponge Cake
Revani (Turkey)

A classic holiday dessert—especially for weddings.

1 cup Thin Syrup, page 134
1 cup unsalted butter or
   margarine, room temperature
1 cup sugar

1 cup semolina
4 eggs
Whole blanched almonds for
   garnish

Prepare Thin Syrup. Set aside to cool. Preheat oven to 350F (175C). Generously grease an 8-inch square baking pan. Set aside. Combine butter or margarine and sugar in a large bowl. Beat until light and fluffy. Gradually add semolina. Beat until blended. Add eggs, one at a time, beating well after each addition. Turn into prepared pan. Bake 30 minutes or until golden. Cut into 2-inch squares or diamond shapes without removing from pan. Press an almond into the center of each piece. Pour half the cooled syrup over warm cake. Let stand

10 minutes or until syrup is absorbed. Pour remaining syrup over cake. Let stand 20 minutes before serving. Makes 12 servings.

Variations

✳ Arabic Sponge Cake: Add 1/2 cup coarsely chopped blanched almonds or 1 cup shredded unsweetened coconut to batter.

✳ Cheese-Filled Sponge Cake: In a small bowl, mix 2 cups ricotta cheese, 1/4 cup sugar and 1 teaspoon orange-blossom water. Mix well. Pour half the cake batter into a greased 11" x 7" baking pan. Cover with cheese mixture. Top with remaining batter. Bake and continue with recipe as directed.

French Cigarettes
Cigarettes au Miel (Tunisia)

These honey-dipped pastries were shared by Mrs. Robert Robaire.

*Almond Paste, page 133, or
    2 cups marzipan
1 tablespoon grated orange peel
Honey Syrup, page 135
1 (1-lb.) pkg. wonton wrappers,
    about 75 skins (3-1/2-inch
    squares)*

*Oil for frying
1/2 cup coarsely chopped
    pistachios, blanched almonds
    or walnuts*

Prepare Almond Paste, if using. Place Almond Paste or marzipan in a medium bowl. Stir in orange peel. Prepare Honey Syrup. Set aside to cool. Place 1 tablespoon Almond Paste or marzipan across bottom of 1 wonton wrapper to within 1/4 inch of sides. Fold edges in 1/2 inch. Roll up jelly-roll fashion. Moisten seams to seal well. Pour oil 1 inch deep into a medium skillet. Heat oil to 350F (175C) on a deep-fry thermometer. At this temperature, a 1-inch cube of bread will turn brown in 65 seconds. Carefully place rolls in hot oil. Do not crowd in skillet. Fry until golden, about 3 minutes. Remove from hot oil. Drain on paper towels. Place in a shallow dish or large baking sheet with rimmed sides in a single layer. Pour cooled syrup over pastries. Let stand 1 hour. Sprinkle with pistachios, almonds or walnuts. Makes 75 rolls.

Variation

✱ Israeli Cigars: Substitute the following filling for Almond Paste or marzipan: Combine 2 cups ground almonds or unsalted peanuts, 2 tablespoons sugar and 1 teaspoon cinnamon. Mix well.

Wedding Cakes
Kourabiedes (Greece)

These cookies are part of almost every cook's holiday repertoire.

*1 cup unsalted butter or
   margarine, room temperature*
1/4 cup granulated sugar
1 egg yolk
*2 tablespoons brandy or orange
   juice, if desired*
*2-1/2 cups sifted all-purpose
   flour*

1/2 teaspoon baking powder
*1/2 cup ground blanched
   almonds (about 2 oz.)*
*About 30 whole cloves,
   if desired*
Powdered sugar for sprinkling

Combine butter or margarine and granulated sugar in a large bowl. Beat in egg yolk until mixture is smooth and light. Beat in brandy or orange juice, if desired. Sift together flour and baking powder. Add to egg mixture, a little at a time, beating well after each addition. Stir in almonds. Turn out onto a floured surface. Knead with floured hands until dough is no longer sticky. Preheat oven to 350F (175C). Pinch off pieces of dough 1 inch in diameter. Shape into balls or crescent shapes. If desired, insert 1 whole clove in center of each ball or crescent. Or use your fingers to press 1 or 2 dimples into each cookie. Place on ungreased baking sheets. Bake 30 to 35 minutes or until cookies are pale golden. Cool on baking sheets. Sprinkle heavily with powdered sugar while still warm. Cookies are extremely fragile. Remove from baking sheets with a spatula. Store in an airtight container between sheets of waxed paper. Makes about 30 cookies.

Penelope Twists
Koulouria (Greece)

Melt-in-your-mouth cookie twists are served during the holidays.

1 cup unsalted butter or
   margarine, room temperature
1/2 cup sugar
1/4 cup vegetable oil
2 eggs
3 tablespoons Cognac or brandy

1/2 teaspoon vanilla extract
3-1/2 cups all-purpose flour
1-1/2 teaspoons baking powder
2 tablespoons orange juice
1 egg, beaten
Sesame seeds for garnish

Place butter or margarine and sugar in a large bowl. Beat until pale and creamy. Add oil. Beat until blended. Add 2 eggs, one at a time. Beat until smooth. Stir in Cognac or brandy and vanilla. Sift together flour and baking powder. Gradually add to egg mixture alternately with orange juice, beating until mixture is smooth. Knead by hand until dough is soft and pliable. Preheat oven to 350F (175C). Butter baking sheets. Pinch off pieces of dough 1 inch in diameter. Shape into balls. Roll each ball between your palms into a 6-inch rope. Fold in center. Hold each end and twist. Place on prepared baking sheets. Brush with beaten egg. Sprinkle with sesame seeds. Bake 20 to 25 minutes or until golden. Makes 16 to 20 twists.

Persian Almond Rolls
Baklava (Iran)

Cardamom and almonds give easy dessert rolls a typically Persian flavor.

Medium Syrup, page 134
2 cups finely chopped blanched
almonds (about 10 oz.)
1 teaspoon ground cardamom
1/4 cup sugar

16 filo pastry sheets
1/2 cup unsalted butter,
clarified, page 129, or
margarine, melted

Prepare Medium Syrup. Set aside to cool. In a small bowl, combine almonds, cardamom and sugar. Set aside. Preheat oven to 350F (175C). Butter a large baking sheet. Stack filo pastry sheets on a flat surface. Cover with plastic wrap to prevent drying out. Stack 2 filo sheets, brushing each with clarified butter or melted margarine. Sprinkle 1/4 cup almond mixture across filo sheets 3 inches from bottom to within 1 inch of sides. Fold in sides. Fold bottom over almond mixture. Roll up jelly-roll fashion. Place on prepared baking sheet. Brush top with butter or margarine. Repeat with remaining filo sheets, butter or margarine and almond mixture. Bake 30 to 35 minutes or until crisp and golden. Pour cooled syrup over warm pastry. Let stand several hours, turning occasionally to coat pastry with syrup. Cut rolls into 2-inch diagonal slices. Makes 8 rolls or about 30 pieces.

Fried Curls
Deples (Greece)

Crisp honey-dipped fried cookies are similar to Italian *crostoli* and Chinese bow ties.

Honey Syrup, see below
1 cup coarsely chopped walnuts
(about 5 oz.)
2 tablespoons sugar
1/4 teaspoon ground cinnamon
3 eggs
1 teaspoon lemon juice
1/2 teaspoon baking powder
1-1/2 to 1-3/4 cups all-purpose
flour

Oil for frying

Honey Syrup:
1 cup honey
1/2 cup water
1 small cinnamon stick
1 teaspoon grated orange peel or
lemon peel
1/2 teaspoon lemon juice

Prepare Honey Syrup. Set aside to cool. In a small bowl, combine walnuts, sugar and cinnamon. Set aside. Beat eggs in a large bowl. Add lemon juice and baking powder. Mix until blended. Gradually add flour until dough pulls away from side of bowl. Flour your hands and knead dough until smooth and no longer sticky. Divide into 4 equal portions. Shape each portion into a ball. Cover with a dry cloth towel. Use a rolling pin or pasta machine to roll out each portion of dough into a paper-thin 30" x 4" strip. If using pasta machine, roll in settings suggested by manufacturer for paper-thin dough. Cut dough into 6" x 4" strips. Cover with towel until ready to fry. Pour oil 1-1/2 inches deep into a large shallow saucepan or skillet. Heat oil to 375F (190C) on a deep-fry thermometer. At this temperature, a 1-inch cube of bread will turn golden brown in 50 seconds. Working with 1 dough strip at a time, carefully place in hot oil. Curl strip around a fork, using another fork as a guide. Cook and turn until curled strip is crisp and golden. Drain on paper towels. Cool. Dip 1 curl at a time into cooled syrup. Drain on a rack over waxed paper. Sprinkle with walnut mixture. Makes 20 cookies.

Honey Syrup:
Combine all ingredients in a small saucepan. Bring to a boil. Reduce heat. Cook, uncovered, over medium heat 10 minutes. Pour into a small bowl.

Filo with Cream Filling
Galaktoboureko (Greece)

I bought this popular pastry at fast-food counters in Boston at Faneuil Hall Market Place.

Medium Syrup, page 134
8 egg yolks
1-1/2 cups sugar
6 cups warm milk (1-1/2 qts.)
6 tablespoons cornstarch
1 cup whipping cream

1 tablespoon vanilla extract
*12 filo pastry sheets
    (about 1/2 lb.)*
*1/2 cup unsalted butter,
    clarified, page 129, or
    margarine, melted*

Prepare Medium Syrup. Set aside to cool. Preheat oven to 350F (175C). Lightly butter a 13" x 9" baking pan. Set aside. Combine egg yolks and sugar in a 2-quart saucepan. Beat until thickened and pale. Stir in warm milk alternately with cornstarch. Stir constantly over low heat until mixture simmers and begins to thicken. Remove from heat. Stir in cream and vanilla. Stir until blended. Stack filo pastry sheets on a flat surface. Trim or fold to fit baking pan. Cover with plastic wrap to prevent drying out. Layer half the filo in pan, brushing each sheet with clarified butter or melted margarine. Pour cream mixture over layers. Top with remaining filo, brushing each sheet with butter or margarine. Brush top sheet with butter or margarine. Lightly score in 2-inch diamond or square shapes with a sharp knife. Do not cut all the way through. Bake 40 to 50 minutes or until golden brown. Pour cooled syrup over warm pastry. Let stand until custard is set. Makes about 24 pieces.

Clarified Butter: Place butter in a skillet over low heat until melted. Simmer over low heat until the milky residue disappears and butter is clear and shiny, about 15 minutes. Skim off any milky residue. Use clarified butter as directed in recipe. Can be kept refrigerated for several weeks.

Deluxe Baklava
(Greek-Style)

My daughter, Marya, prepares this luxurious baklava as a Christmas gift for special friends.

Medium Syrup, page 134
4 cups finely chopped walnuts
   (about 1-1/4 lbs.)
1 tablespoon ground cinnamon
1/2 teaspoon ground allspice
1/2 teaspoon ground nutmeg
1/4 teaspoon ground cloves

1/4 cup sugar
40 filo pastry sheets
   (about 2 lbs.)
1-1/2 cups unsalted butter,
   clarified, above, or
   margarine, melted

Prepare Medium Syrup. Set aside to cool. Preheat oven to 350F (175C). Lightly butter a 13" x 9" baking pan. Set aside. In a medium bowl, combine walnuts, cinnamon, allspice, nutmeg, cloves and sugar. Set aside. Stack filo pastry sheets on a flat surface. Trim to fit pan. Cover with plastic wrap to prevent drying out. Layer 12 filo sheets in baking pan, brushing each sheet with clarified butter or melted margarine. Spread 1 cup nut mixture over layered filo sheets. Top with 8 more filo sheets, brushing each with butter or margarine. Spread with 1 cup nut mixture. Layer 8 more filo sheets, brushing each with butter or margarine. Spread with remaining nut mixture. Top with 12 remaining filo sheets, brushing each with butter or margarine. Brush top sheet with remaining butter or margarine. Cutting all the way through pastry, cut into 1-inch diamond shapes without removing from pan. Bake 30 minutes. Reduce heat to 200F (95C). Bake 30 minutes longer. Pour cooled syrup over warm pastry. Let stand several hours before serving. Makes about 110 pieces.

Butter Rings
Graybeh (Syria)

Julie Nassraway's tender cookies won't overcook when baked on double baking sheets (air-cell bottom).

3 cups all-purpose flour	*About 1-1/4 cups butter or*
1-1/2 cups fine-grade semolina	*margarine, room temperature*
Dash of salt	*24 to 30 toasted whole blanched*
1 cup sugar	*almonds, page 46*

Preheat oven to 250F (120C). Place 1 baking sheet on top of another. Set aside. Combine flour, semolina, salt and sugar in a large bowl. Mix well. Add 1 cup butter or margarine. Beat with electric mixer, adding more butter or margarine to make a soft pliable dough. Knead dough with your hands until no longer sticky. Pinch off 1-inch pieces. Roll each piece with your palms on a clean surface to make an 8-inch rope. Form into a circle, overlapping ends. Press an almond into over-lapping ends to fasten. Place on ungreased double baking sheets. Bake

20 minutes. Increase temperature to 350F (175C). Bake 10 minutes longer or until cookies are firm, but not brown. They should be slightly golden underneath. Makes 24 to 30 cookies.

☼ Clotted Cream
Kaymak (Turkey)

A simplified version of the cream used to garnish sweet pastries. It closely resembles Devonshire cream.

1 cup dairy sour cream | *2 cups whipping cream*

   Place sour cream in a large bowl. Stir until smooth. Gradually stir in whipping cream until blended. Cover with a clean cloth. Let stand at cool room temperature (65F, 20C) 24 hours. Line a bowl with several paper coffee filters or triple layers of cheesecloth with enough overhang to lift out easily. Transfer cream mixture to prepared bowl. Cover with a clean cloth. Refrigerate 24 hours. Cream will separate from whey. Lift cream out of bowl using overhanging filters or cheesecloth. Place on a plate. Spoon cream into a refrigerator container. Cover and refrigerate. May be stored up to 1 week. Makes 2 cups.

☼ Yogurt Cheese
Labanah (Arabic)

A traditional breakfast: sprinkle Yogurt Cheese with olive oil and serve with olives and pocket bread.

2 cups plain yogurt or Homemade Yogurt, page 132 | *1 teaspoon salt*

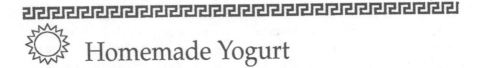

Fold a large piece of cheesecloth into a square several thicknesses thick. Or use a clean, white, lint-free towel. Place yogurt in center of cheesecloth square or towel. Bring corners up and tie securely, making a bag containing yogurt. Hang bag from faucet over a bowl several hours or overnight at cool temperature. Or place bag in a colander over a bowl and let stand in refrigerator at room temperature several hours or overnight. Remove cheese from bag. Place in a medium bowl. Stir in salt. Place in a refrigerator container. Cover and refrigerate. Use within 1 week. Makes about 3/4 cup.

☀ Homemade Yogurt

Choose one of several methods for making yogurt easily and inexpensively at home.

4 cups nonfat, low-fat or regular milk (1 qt.) | *2 tablespoons plain yogurt*

Heat milk in a 2-quart saucepan to 185F (85C) or until bubbles appear around edges. Let cool to 110F (45C), lukewarm. Place yogurt in a small bowl. Stir about 1/2 cup lukewarm milk into yogurt. Pour yogurt mixture into milk, stirring gently to blend. Do not stir vigorously or mixture will become tart. If using a yogurt maker, follow manufacturer's instructions. If using a thermos bottle, fill with warm water 115F (45C). Discard water and refill thermos with yogurt mixture, Replace cap and let stand 4 hours. If using a saucepan or ceramic or plastic bowl, rinse in warm water. Place yogurt mixture in pan or bowl. Cover with lid or plastic wrap. Cover completely with a double-thickness of bath towel. Keep covered at least 6 hours or until yogurt is set. If using oven, preheat to 150F (65C). Turn off heat. Cover yogurt and place in warm oven. Let stand several hours or overnight. Cool. Store yogurt in refrigerator. Makes 1 quart. (See next page for variations.)

Variations

✳ Rich Yogurt: Substitute 2 cups whipping cream (1 pint) for 2 cups of the milk.

✳ Fruit Yogurt: Sweeten 1-1/2 cups pureed or mashed fruit with 1/4 cup sugar. Blend in 1 teaspoon lemon juice. Stir into Homemade Yogurt.

Almond Paste

Dhaw'k Allawz (Arabic)

The Arabs take credit for this confection used to fill dates, pastries and cookies.

1 cup blanched almonds
1-1/2 cups powdered sugar
1 large egg white

2 teaspoons almond extract
2 or 3 drops rose water

Preheat oven to 300F (150C). Spread almonds on a baking sheet. Bake 10 to 15 minutes or until almonds appear oily but not browned. Cool slightly. Place almonds in blender or food processor. Process until ground. Add powdered sugar, egg white and almond extract. Process until a paste is formed. Add rose water. Process a few seconds longer. Scrape side of container with a rubber spatula. Turn paste into a plastic or glass container. Cover and refrigerate 4 days to blend flavors. May be stored up to 4 months. Makes 1 cup.

Thin Syrup

Thin syrups are usually poured over sponge cakes. Try one of the flavored variations.

3 cups sugar
4 cups water (1 qt.)

1/2 lemon

Combine all ingredients in a large, heavy saucepan. Bring to a boil, stirring frequently. Reduce heat. Once mixture boils and sugar is dissolved, do not stir or syrup may cloud or crystallize. Cook, uncovered, over medium-low heat until a candy thermometer registers 205F (95C). At this temperature, syrup dropped from a cold metal spoon will fall in a thin stream. Discard lemon half. Cool syrup. Use immediately or refrigerate in a plastic container with lid. May be refrigerated up to 1 month. Makes 3 cups.

Variations
✳ Cinnamon Thin Syrup: Add 1 cinnamon stick with lemon half.
✳ Rose-Water Thin Syrup: Stir 1/2 teaspoon rose water into cooked syrup.
✳ Orange-Blossom Thin Syrup: Stir 1/2 teaspoon orange-blossom water into cooked syrup.

Medium Syrup

This syrup is most commonly used on baklava and other sweet filo pastries.

3 cups sugar
1-1/2 cups water

2 tablespoons lemon juice

Combine all ingredients in a large, heavy saucepan. Bring to a boil, stirring frequently. Reduce heat. Once mixture boils and sugar is dissolved, do not stir or syrup may cloud or crystallize. Cook, uncovered, over medium-low heat until a candy thermometer registers 212 to 218F (100 to 102C). At this temperature, syrup dropped from a cold metal spoon will fall in a sheet. Remove from heat. Cool. Use immediately or refrigerate in a plastic container with lid. May be refrigerated up to 1 month. Makes about 2 cups.

Variations

* Honey Syrup: Stir in 2 tablespoons honey after removing from heat.
* Rose-Water Medium Syrup: Stir 1/2 teaspoon rose water into cooked syrup.
* Orange-Blossom Medium Syrup: Stir 1/2 teaspoon orange-blossom water into cooked syrup.

Turkish Delight
Lokum (Turkey)

Somewhat different from what you buy in candy stores but equally delicious.

3 envelopes unflavored gelatin
1/2 cup water
2 cups granulated sugar
1 cup water

1 cup citrus, apple or
*   pomegranate juice*
Food coloring, if desired
Powdered sugar

Oil an 8-inch square pan. Dissolve gelatin in 1/2 cup water. In a medium saucepan, combine granulated sugar and 1 cup water. Bring to a boil over medium heat. Add dissolved-gelatin mixture. Stir until blended. Simmer over low heat 30 minutes. Add fruit juice. Add food coloring, if desired. Simmer 5 minutes longer. Pour into prepared pan. Refrigerate until firm. Use a sharp, wet knife to cut into 1-inch cubes. Spread powdered sugar on a large piece of waxed paper. Drop cubes onto powdered sugar and toss to coat well. Makes 64 pieces.

Sesame Candy
Pastelli (Greece)

This candy has been made in many Middle Eastern countries for thousands of years.

1 (1-lb.) jar honey (2 cups) | *1 lb. hulled sesame seeds*

Butter an 11" x 7" square pan. Set aside. Heat honey in a medium saucepan over medium heat until a candy thermometer registers 280F (140C). At this temperature, syrup dropped into cold water will separate into threads which are hard but not brittle. Stir in sesame seeds. Immediately pour into prepared pan. Cool slightly. While still soft, cut into diagonal 2" x 1" strips or diamond shapes. Do not remove from pan until candy is firm. Makes about 40 pieces.

Preserved Grape Leaves
Warak Arish Makboos (Arabic)

Preserve your own grape leaves for Meat-Stuffed Grape Leaves, page 20.

50 to 70 grape leaves | *Lemon wedges*
8 cups water (2 qts.) | *3 cups water*
1/4 cup salt | *3 cups vinegar*

Sterilize two 1-quart canning jars and lids according to manufacturer's instructions. Rinse grape leaves. Use only young leaves that have not been exposed to chemicals or pesticides. Pour 8 cups water into a large saucepan. Add salt. Bring to a boil. Add grape leaves. Boil 30 seconds. Drain, discarding water in pan. Let leaves stand until cool enough to handle. Place leaves shiny-sides up in stacks of 10 to 15 with largest leaves on bottom. Roll up each stack and tie with string. Pack vertically into hot sterilized jars. Trim edges of rolls to fit jar, if necessary. Tuck in several lemon wedges. Pour 3 cups water and 3 cups vinegar into a large saucepan. Bring to a boil. Pour over leaves in jars, covering completely. Seal jars according to manufacturer's instructions. May be stored in refrigerator up to 6 months. For longer storage, process filled jars 15 minutes in a hot-water bath, at right, according to manufacturer's instructions. Makes about 2 quarts.

Use a hot-water bath for canning fruits, tomatoes and other acidic foods, butters, conserves, preserves and jams. The foods must be immersed in boiling water (212F, 100C) in a canner or large kettle. Process from 10 to 45 minutes, depending on the type of food and size of jars.

Preserved Lemons or Limes
Citron Confits à la Marocaine (Morocco)

Preserved citrus fruits add zest and flavor to Lemon Chicken, page 105, or to a favorite stew.

10 ripe medium lemons or limes (about 3 lbs.)	*1 tablespoon coriander seeds*
4 to 5 tablespoons salt	*1 teaspoon whole cloves*
	About 8 cups water (2 qts.)

Sterilize canning jars and lids according to manufacturer's instructions. Wide-mouthed jars are necessary to accommodate whole lemons. Make a deep slit on 4 sides of each fruit, starting from bottom and ending short of stem end, so cut fruit will keep its shape. Sprinkle salt into slits, making sure salt is packed in well. Place fruit in hot sterilized jars. Divide coriander seeds and cloves evenly among jars. Pour 8 cups water into a saucepan. Bring to a boil. Pour as much boiling water over fruit in jars as needed to cover fruit completely. If necessary, weight down fruit with a sterilized stone to keep submerged. Seal jars according to manufacturer's instructions. Store in a cool, dark, dry place 3 weeks before using. May be stored up to 6 months. For longer storage, process filled jars 20 minutes in a hot-water bath, page 137, according to manufacturer's instructions. To use Preserved Lemons or Limes, skim off harmless residue on top of liquid. Use tongs to remove required amount of fruit. Wash fruit and cut into quarters to eat as pickles. To flavor stews and other foods, remove and discard pulp and use only peel. Makes 2 quarts.

 # Marinated Greek Olives
Elies Marinates (Greece)

Plain cured olives dressed up with spices and vegetables.

1 qt. canned pitted or unpitted, black or green olives	1 leek stalk, white part only, sliced
1 cup olive oil	2 orange slices
1/2 cup red-wine vinegar	1 lemon, sliced
1 teaspoon crushed dried-leaf oregano	2 small hot red peppers
	1 bay leaf

Make a slit in 1 side of each olive. Place in a large clean bowl or jar. Add remaining ingredients. Mix well. Cover. Marinate several hours before eating. Place in jars to store. It is not necessary to seal jars. Olives may be stored in refrigerator up to 1 month. Makes 1 quart.

☼ Black Pepper Spice
Huwait (Yemen)

Add all-purpose Yemenite spice to soups, sauces and even yogurt.

2 tablespoons freshly ground
black pepper

2 tablespoons ground turmeric
1 tablespoon ground cumin

Combine all ingredients in a jar with a tight-fitting lid. Shake to mix well. May be stored up to 1 year. Makes about 1/4 cup.

☼ Mixed Spice
Baharat (Arabic)

Arab housewives purchase this all-purpose spice mix by the bagful.

2 tablespoons freshly ground
pepper
1 tablespoon ground coriander
1 tablespoon ground cloves

2 tablespoons ground cumin
1/2 teaspoon ground cardamom
1 nutmeg, grated
Pinch of ground cinnamon

Combine all ingredients in a jar with a tight-fitting lid. Shake to mix well. May be stored up to 1 year. Makes about 1/2 cup.

INDEX

Regional Index

Many of the recipes in this book have crossed regional boundaries. The following classifications are given as a guide to recipe origins.

Arabic

Iranian

Israeli

Near Eastern

North African

Yemen